NUMEROLOGY

MULANK, BHAGYANK, ANGEL NUMBERS, NAME NUMEROLOGY AND MOBILE PHONE NUMBER NUMEROLOGY

DR. YADUVIR SINGH

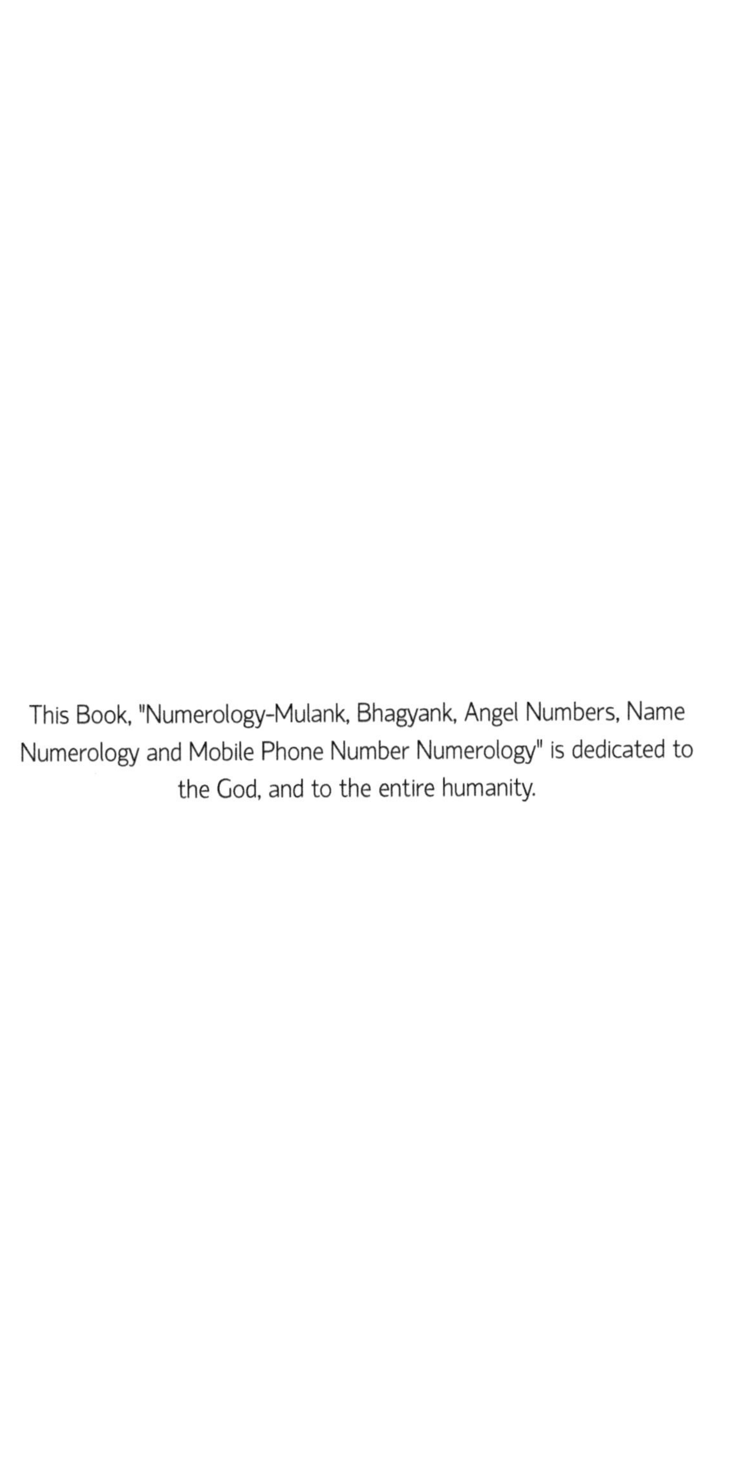

This Book, "Numerology-Mulank, Bhagyank, Angel Numbers, Name Numerology and Mobile Phone Number Numerology" is dedicated to the God, and to the entire humanity.

Contents

Contents

Foreword

This Book, "Numerology-Mulank, Bhagyank, Angel Numbers, Name Numerology and Mobile Phone Number Numerology" is a treatise on Numerology. Numbers are the Symbols, and the Symbols have Powers. Numerology is the Language of Numbers. Numbers communicate with us, and are the tools of the Numerology. Numerology is a branch of the Astrology. Every event of the life is influenced by the Navagrahas, or simply the 9 Planets. Surya or Sun, Chandra or Moon, Rahu and Ketu, are quite significant for knowing the self.

This Book, "Numerology-Mulank, Bhagyank, Angel Numbers, Name Numerology and Mobile Phone Number Numerology", has very beautifully, and in a very lucid manner, dealt with the inner aspects of the Numerology, like Mulank, Bhagyank, Angel Numbers, Name Numerology, Mobile Phone Number Numerology, Vehicle Registration Number Numerology etc.. A mere reading of this Book will definitely help the reader in shaping his or her future, and turning the situations and the events of his or her life in his or her favour and benefit.

There are various occult and mystical reasons of not getting success or becoming rich, or gaining a position and power, despite the hard work; the reason is non-compatibility of the numbers. Align the energies of numbers with the help of numerology, and then, even a simple work done, will reap the intended benefits. Here in this inexplicable creation, all and everything is energy. Numerology is energy alignment through the numbers. Numbers are the tools for this purpose.

Author's knowledge and the experience of Vaastu has further value-added the contents of this Book, "Numerology-Mulank, Bhagyank, Angel Numbers, Name Numerology and Mobile Phone Number Numerology". Readers will find this Book, "Numerology-Mulank, Bhagyank, Angel Numbers, Name Numerology and Mobile Phone Number Numerology", quite interesting and useful. This Book, "Numerology-Mulank, Bhagyank, Angel Numbers, Name Numerology and Mobile Phone Number Numerology" has many takeaways for their direct implementation in our daily life.

This Book, "Numerology-Mulank, Bhagyank, Angel Numbers, Name Numerology and Mobile Phone Number Numerology" is a treasure trove, a very precious gift to the entire humanity by the author. The author has done his devoir right well.

-**Baba**
22/03/2024

Preface

This Book on Numerology, contains the World of Numbers, is perfectly fitting in your hands; dang, not knowing it.

This Book, "Numerology-Mulank, Bhagyank, Angel Numbers, Name Numerology and Mobile Phone Number Numerology" is a masterpiece of Numerology. There are various occult and mystical reasons of not getting success or becoming rich, or gaining a position and power, despite the hard work; the reason is non-compatibility of the numbers. Align the energies of numbers with the help of numerology, and then, even a simple work done, will reap the intended benefits and the results. Everything is energy here. This creation is a play of energy and matter (or material). Stating plainly, Numerology is the energy alignment with the help of numbers. Numbers are the elements of Yantra and Trantra, and to some extent of Mantra. Numerology is the Language of Numbers. Numbers are the Symbols, and the Symbols have Powers. Numbers communicate with us, and are the tools of the Numerology. Numerology is a branch of the Astrology. Every event of the life is influenced by the Navagrahas, or simply the 9 Planets. Surya or Sun, Chandra or Moon, Rahu and Ketu, are quite significant for knowing the self.

This Book, "Numerology-Mulank, Bhagyank, Angel Numbers, Name Numerology and Mobile Phone Number Numerology", has very beautifully, and in a very lucid manner, dealt with the inner aspects of the Numerology, like Mulank, Bhagyank, Angel Numbers, Name Numerology, Mobile Phone Number Numerology, Vehicle Registration Number Numerology etc.. A mere reading of this Book will definitely help the reader in shaping his or her future, and turning the situations and the events of his or her life in his or her favour and benefit.

This Book, "Numerology-Mulank, Bhagyank, Angel Numbers, Name Numerology and Mobile Phone Number Numerology", is a great gift from the author to the entire humanity in today's tough times. This Book, "Numerology-Mulank, Bhagyank, Angel Numbers, Name Numerology and Mobile Phone Number Numerology", is a best pick of its times, from e-commerce platforms and bookstores, and a must read for all. This Book, "Numerology-Mulank, Bhagyank, Angel Numbers, Name Numerology and Mobile Phone Number Numerology", is a guide for the life. I wish all the readers, a happy reading, and exciting and enriching reading experience, while going through, every word, every line, every paragraph, and every chapter of this Book. Readers will find this Book, too involving, and there will be an evolving experience. Readers will not be able to stop reading this Book, and repeat, reading this Book, time and again. Read and explain the contents of this Book to your family members, friends, relatives and colleagues. Gift this Book, "Numerology-Mulank, Bhagyank, Angel Numbers, Name Numerology and Mobile Phone Number Numerology", to your well-wishers. A gift of knowledge is always the best gift.

-**Dr. Yaduvir Singh**
25/02/2024

Acknowledgements

Author will like to acknowledge the Universe, its energies, various sources of information and inspiration, and all the wise and experienced people of present and past times. Nothing is possible without God's will. Author, will full servility, respect and the gratitude, surrenders to the God, and puts this Book, "Numerology-Mulank, Bhagyank, Angel Numbers, Name Numerology and Mobile Phone Number Numerology", on the holy feet of the God.

All is of the God only.

Reading this Book, and following its contents in the Life, are purely reader's choice, and there will be no liability and the responsibility on the Author, or the Publisher, of any kind. Contents have been taken from various sources, including the Author's life's learning, personal beliefs and the experiences. What happens with the one may not happen in the Life at all with the others. Reader's full discretion is needed, while reading and following the contents of this Book. The Author shall not be responsible in any way for any negative consequences arising thereof. It is the matter of one's faith and belief. Author disclaims all the responsibilities and the liabilities, arising after reading this Book. Purchase, reading and implementing the contents of this Book, is purely, a matter of reader's choice only, with no liabilities and responsibilities of any kind on the Author. One may completely disagree with everything written in this Book. Author does not want to hurt the sentiments and the beliefs of anybody. Author submits his apologies in advance in all such cases. Author believes in the power of numbers, therefore, his free personal views are expressed in his this

Book. One may totally disagree with the contents herein, and refute everything as written here in this Book. Today, there is need for the tolerance. The reactions and responses to anything must lie within certain limits and the boundaries. Why to fight? Why to hate? No other person is enemy of self, but we ourselves are our enemies. Life is all about the right perspective. Human dignity must be upheld in every case, no matter what. God made this world and us to live in harmony, joyfully and peacefully. Nobody is going to stay here, nor any problem. Nothing is for real here. All is an illusion here. My sincere apologies in advance, if anybody's emotions and sentiments are hurt in any manner. Read this book with openness and free mind, and purely on your personal choice and responsibility.

DISCLAIMER:

Reader(s) may totally disagree with the contents of this Book on Numerology. Every subject or topic is the matter of one's religion, faith and belief, and the experiences. Author believes in Numerology, therefore, he has authored this Book. Author will not be responsible for any liability or responsibility or the negative consequences associated with this Book's contents and their reading and implementation. Reader's full discretion is needed here. Reading and implementing this Book's contents is purely the choice of the reader. In no way, Author will be responsible for anything.

Prologue

This Book, "Numerology-Mulank, Bhagyank, Angel Numbers, Name Numerology and Mobile Phone Number Numerology" is a masterpiece of Numerology. There are various occult and mystical reasons of not getting success or becoming rich, or gaining a position and power, despite the hard work; the reason is non-compatibility of the numbers. Align the energies of numbers with the help of numerology, and then, even a simple work done, will reap the intended benefits and the results. Everything is energy here. This creation is a play of energy and matter (or material). Stating plainly, Numerology is the energy alignment with the help of numbers. Numbers are the elements of Yantra and Trantra, and to some extent of Mantra. Numerology is the Language of Numbers. Numbers are the Symbols, and the Symbols have Powers. Numbers communicate with us, and are the tools of the Numerology. Numerology is a branch of the Astrology. Every event of the life is influenced by the Navagrahas, or simply the 9 Planets. Surya or Sun, Chandra or Moon, Rahu and Ketu, are quite significant for knowing the self.

There are various occult and mystical reasons of not getting success or becoming rich, or gaining a position and power, despite the hard work; the reason is non-compatibility of the numbers. Align the energies of numbers with the help of numerology, and then, even a simple work done, will reap the intended benefits. Here in this inexplicable creation, all and everything is energy. Numerology is energy alignment through the numbers. Numbers are the tools for this purpose.

This Book, "Numerology-Mulank, Bhagyank, Angel Numbers, Name Numerology and Mobile Phone Number Numerology", contains the World of Numbers, is perfectly fitting in your hands; dang, not knowing it.

Introduction

Numerology is an occult Science, dealing with the Divine and/or the mystical relationships between the numbers and the events of the Life. Numerology studies the relationship between being's Life and the Number(s). Numerology is the Language of Numbers. Numbers communicate with us, and are the tools of the Numerology. Numbers are the Symbols, and the Symbols have Powers. Numerology helps in knowing the Friend-Number(s) of our Psychic Number, and also, in knowing that how these numbers can attract Luck in the Life. Numerology is a branch of the Astrology. Every event of the life is influenced by the Navagrahas, or simply the 9 Planets. Surya or Sun, Chandra or Moon, Rahu and Ketu, are quite significant for knowing the self. Numerology is an applied mysticism, which correlates a mystical symbol with a being's Life. Numbers have psychic abilities. Numerology is all about the Perception. Numerology is also about the Vibrations. Numerology is about the Frequencies. Numbers from 1 to 9, including the 0 (Shunya, origin: India), help in knowing the complete self. Numerology has been well back-tested. Various types of Numerology are the Vedic Numerology, the Lo Shu Grid Numerology (Chinese Numerology), the Pythagorean Numerology, the Chaldean

Numerology, the Tamil Numerology, and the Kabbalah Numerology. The Numbers, and their associated Planets, as per Vedic Numerology are as follows:

Number 0: Pluto

Number 1: Sun (commonly known as the Surya) - Soul

Number 1 represents East Direction and the Fire Element, as per the Vedic Numerology.

Number 1 represents North Direction and the Water Element, as per the Lo Shu Grid Numerology.

Number 2: Moon (commonly known as the Chandrama or Chanda) - Mind

Number 2 represents North-West Direction and the Water Element, as per the Vedic Numerology.

Number 2 represents South-West Direction and the Earth Element, as per the Lo Shu Grid Numerology.

Number 3: Jupiter (commonly known as the Guru) - Sky or Ether or Space

Number 3 represents North-East Direction and the Sky or Ether or Space Element, as per the Vedic Numerology.

Number 3 represents East Direction and the Wood Element, as per the Lo Shu Grid Numerology.

Number 4: Uranus (commonly known as the Rahu) - Material Pursuits

Number 4 represents South-West Direction and the Fire Element, as per the Vedic Numerology.

Number 4 represents Soth-East Direction and the Wood Element, as per the Lo Shu Grid Numerology.

Number 5: Mercury (commonly known as the Buddh) - Air, Earth

Number 5 is the North Direction, and represents the Air and Earth Elements, as per the Vedic Numerology.

Number 5 represents Centre and the Earth Element, as per the Lo Shu Grid Numerology.

Number 6: Venus (commonly known as the Shukra) - Air, Water, Fire and Earth

Number 6 represents South-East Direction and the Air, Water, Fire and Earth Element, as per the Vedic Numerology.

Number 6 represents North-West Direction and the Metal Element, as per the Lo Shu Grid Numerology.

Number 7: Shadow Planet Neptune (commonly known as the Ketu) - Fire, Spiritual Pursuits

Number 7 represents North-East Direction and the Fire Element, as per the Vedic Numerology.

Number 7 represents West Direction and the Metal Element, as per the Lo Shu Grid Numerology.

Number 8: Saturn (commonly known as the Shani) - Air

Number 8 represents West Direction and the Air Element, as per the Vedic Numerology.

Number 8 represents North-East Direction and the Earth Element, as per the Lo Shu Grid Numerology.

and

Number 9: Mars (commonly known as the Mangal) - Fire

Number 9 represents South Direction and the Fire Element, as per the Vedic Numerology.

Number 9 represents South Direction and the Fire Element, as per the Lo Shu Grid Numerology.

Sun is, the King, the Government, the Bureaucracy. Sun refers to Essence and the Leadership. Moon is the Mind. Moon refers to the Emotions. Jupiter refers to Wisdom and the Opportunities. Rahu represents the Hardware. Rahu refers to Karmic Lessons and the Spiritual Liberation. Mercury represents the Intellect. Venus refers to the Aesthetics. Venus or the Shukra, represents goddess Lakshmi, i.e. the goddess of Wealth, Money, Luck and

Fortune. Ketu represents the Software. Ketu refers to Karmic Lessons and the Spiritual Liberation. Saturn refers to Structure and the Discipline. And, Mars refers to the Energy.

Vedic numerology is most ancient. Vedic Numerology has its origin in the Anka Shastra. Vedic Numerology is integral to the Horoscope. Vedic Numerology uses the Numbers, associated with the Planets, for the purpose of calculations, in order to give predictions. According to the Vedic Numerology, Numbers from 1 to 9, including 0 (the Shunya (the void); origin in India) help in knowing the Self, i.e. everything about the Life (events) and the World. In the Vedic Numerology, the Number Zero symbolises the Ego or the Self or the Lagna, i.e. the Innate Intelligence. Planet's degrees or the Positional Indicators are also called as the Shadbala. The Number 0 (Zero), as the Vedic Numerology, embodies deep spiritual and esoteric concepts and interpretations. As per the Vedic Numerology, all the events of the Life are fully influenced by the Navagrahas or the 9 Planets. As per the Vedic Numerology, Chandrama or the Moon is, "the most" significant factor, when it comes to knowing about the Self. In the Vedic Numerology, which is the part of the Vedic Astrology, the Ascending Node and the Descending Node of the Moon are indicated by the Rahu, and the Ketu. Thus, there is significant role of the Rahu and the Ketu in the Life of the being as per the Vedic Numerology.

Pythagorean Numerology is a System of interpreting the meaning of certain Core Numbers in the life. These Core Numbers are calculated from Date of Birth or the Name. The 5 Core Numbers in Pythagorean Numerology are the Life Path Number, the Soul Urge Number, the Expression Number, the Personality Number, and the Birthday

Number. Pythagorean Numerology tells about someone's Character and the Fate. As per the Pythagorean Numerology, the Numbers are Male or Female, and Ugly or Beautiful. As per the Pythagorean Numerology, the Number 1 is the Number of the Reason. Number 2 is the first Even and the Female Number. Number 2 is the Number of the Opinion. Number 3 is the first True Male Number. Number 3 is the Number of the Harmony. When 2 and 3 come together, i.e. 2 + 3 = 5; 5 is the Number of Marriage. All Even Numbers are Female. All Odd Numbers are Male. Number 4 is the Number of the Justice or the Retribution. Number 5 is connected to Mercury. Number 5 is the Number of Wisdom, Fastness, Change, Finance and Communication. The Combination 555 is very powerful number and indicates a major change in the Life. Number 6 is associated with the nurturing energy (Harmony and Balance). Number 6 represents Trust, Love & Care, Art, Romance and Responsibility. Number 7 is the Number of the Occult and the Spirituality. Number 7 is the Luckiest Number. Numbers 1, 5 and 9 beings are capable of handling pressures, and are very good fighters. Numbers 1, 5 and 9 are perfect numbers, and the symbols of success. Numbers 1, 5 and 9 beings are not afraid of unfavourable situations and circumstances of their Life, and are able to bounce back every time. They are the top, very rich and quite powerful beings. Number 8 is the number of Power, Position, Authority, Balance, Abundance, Success and Prosperity. Number 8 is the number of Planet Saturn or the Shani. Shani represents the Career and the Growth in the Life. Shoes and slippers are connected with the Shani. Do not keep old, dirty, torn shoes and slippers in the house; discard these. Keep limited number of Shoes and Slippers. Donate Shoes and Slippers on the Days of the Day of Date of Birth, for a better Career, Success and the Growth. It is powerful remedy for making Shani happy for benefit. Number 9 is the number of Completion (Positive Energy, Learning, Growth, Selflessness, Humanitarianism and the Good Luck). Number 10 is the most perfect number because 10 = 1 + 2 + 3 + 4.

There are 03 categories of Numbers in the Numerology, viz. the Virtuous (सात्विकि), the Majestic (राजसकि or रजोगुणी), and the Vengeful (तामसकि or तमोगुणी). Virtuous Numbers are 1, 3, 5 and 7. Majestic Numbers are 2 and 6. And, the Vengeful Numbers are 4, 8 and 9. Rahu, Shukra and Shani, i.e. Numbers 4, 6 and 8, have ability to make beings extremely Rich in their Life. Guru, i.e. Number 3 is very good for Knowledge in the Life. Rahu, Ketu and Shukra give Luxury in the Life. 4 is the Number of Brain (logic, reasoning etc.). Numbers 3 and 6 create a very bad combination.

Number 1 is the number of the Leader, i.e. the King. Number 2 is the number of Love and Emotion. Number 2 is the number of the Queen. Numbers 1 and 2 are the best combination, i.e. made for each other; the King and the Queen. In the Numerology, number 3 is the number of joy. Number 3 is associated with optimism, communication, creativity and curiosity. Number 3 is a creative communicator. Number 4 in the Numerology, is associated with the practicality, stability and a very strong sense of order. Number 4 beings are, practical, organized, quite hard-working, traditional, dependable and loyal, but emotional, non-adaptive and over-thinkers and over-analyst. Number 5 is the number of Balance. Number 9 is the number of Courage. Beings having 1, 5 and 9 are very strong decision makers, and also, implementers. Beings having 1, 5 and 9, struggle in their Life nearly up to 30 years of their age, and thereafter, get huge success, name, fame and glory. In the Numerology, numbers 5 and 7 have no enemies. Number 6 is the number of name, fame and money. Number 6 means the Venus, and the Venus is a very beautiful planet. Green Colour is good for Number 6 beings. Number 7 is a spiritual number. Number 8 is the number of logic and money. Number 9 is the number of Bliss, the Enlightenment, the Liberation, the Salvation, i.e. Moksha (Beyond the Body).

In the Vedic Numerology, there are three types of Numbers, viz. Mulank or the Personal Number, Bhagyank or the Destiny Number, and the Name Number. As per the Vedic Numerology, these three Numbers, viz. Personal Number, Destiny Number and the Name Number hold much significance, while assessing the suitability and alignment of dates for important events or the activities of being's Life. Date of Birth contains Mulank and Bhagyank.

Mulank is also called as the Birth Number or the Personality Number or the Psychic Number or the Personal Number. Mulank refers to the being's inner self, i.e. being's mind, soul, and the nature. Mulank indicates hopes, desires, wishes and the ambitions. Mulank is calculated by reducing, only the Day of the Date of Birth of a being, to a single-digit number. Let, the Date of Birth be March 22, 1997. The Day of this Date of Birth is 22, so the Mulank would be 2 + 2 = 4. Hence, Mulank is 4. Mulank has greater impact up to 35 years of the age. In the Vedic Numerology, Psychic Numbers 2, 3, 4, 6, and 8 are considered favourable.

Bhagyank is also called as the Psychic Number or the Destiny Number or the Life Path Number. Bhagyank denotes the factor of Luck in the life. Bhagyank refers to, what one will get in his or her life. Past Lives Karma affect the Bhagyank. Bhagyank denotes the choices in the Life. The Life Path Number uncovers one's Strength, Weaknesses, Challenges, Character, Life Lessons, Goals and Obstacles and Events of the Life. The Life Path Number shows the Path of Life, i.e. the Purpose of Life. Bhagyank is calculated by, first adding all the digits of the Date of Birth, i.e. the Day, the Month, and the Year, and then, reducing the sum to a single-digit number. Let, the Date of Birth be March 22, 1997. The Bhagyank would be ((2 + 2 + 3 + 1 + 9 + 9 + 7 = 33, then 3 + 3 = 6), or ((date+ month + year) = 4 (2 + 2 = 4) + 3 + 8 (1 + 9 + 9 + 7 = 26) = 4 + 3 + 8 = 15 = 1 + 5 = 6)). Hence, Bhagyank is 6. Bhagyank or the Destiny Number gets active after the age of 35 years. Bhagyank or the Destiny Number has a much greater impact after 35 years of the age in the Life. In the Vedic Numerology, Destiny Numbers 1, 5, 7, and 9 are considered quite auspicious. Destiny Number is useful in making important decisions of the Life pertaining to the long-term projects, such as starting a Business, or Investment or Property, or even finding his or her Soulmate. Compatibility in relationships is necessary for Stability, Peace and the Happiness in the Life. Destiny Number helps a being selecting a Career, a compatible Partner for the purpose of Marriage or the Love Relationships. Destiny cannot be changed; however, measures can always be taken to improve the Life by mitigating the problems and reducing the intensity of sufferings. Make the most out of the Numbers, with the help of the Numerology.

Mulank and the Bhagyank must be in harmony for a Happy Life.

Name Number is the being's eternal link to the external material world, even after the Death. Name Number is calculated by, adding the numerical values assigned to each letter of being's full name (first, middle, and the last names). These numerical values as recommended in Vedic Numerology are as follows:

A, I, J, Q, Y = 1

B, C, K, R = 2

G, L, S = 3

D, M, T = 4

N, E = 5

U, V, W, X = 6

O, Z = 7

F, H, P = 8

There is no Number 9 for Name Numerology as per the Vedic Numerology. Harmony between the Psychic Number and the Destiny Number, if these are same, plays a substantial role in being's Life and the day-to-day Decision-making. Being's Psychic Number and the Destiny Number appear in certain area(s) on his or her Horoscope.

Angel Numbers are also called as the Kuan Numbers or the K-Numbers. K-Number is the Number of Luck and Blessings in the Life. K Number shows the Direction in the Life, i.e., What to do, What not to do, etc., in the Life. K-Number gives strength to the beings. Angel Numbers or Kuan Numbers or the K-Numbers are a Sign from the God that you're on the right track of the Life, i.e. the Directionality. Angel Numbers appear in the most ordinary places or the spaces, at certain divinely ordered times of the Life, and definitely grab being's Attention. Angel Numbers evoke a Sense of Wonder. Within the Numerology, the Angel Numbers are, simply three to four numbers, repetitive number sequences like, 222 or 4444, and/or, interesting patterns like 123 or 321 or 6767 or 8787 or 9889. Angel Numbers, also offer Insights and the Wisdom.

Appearance of Angel Numbers is a cosmic nudge, affirming that whatever is happening in the Life, has a much bigger purpose, and a new beginning is imminent. Finding one's K-Number is very easy. Consider only the Year of Birth, e.g., 1997. 1997 totals to 8 (1+9+9+7 = 26 = 2+6 = 8). For males, K-Number is obtained by subtracting this total from 11. In this case, it is 11-8 = 3. Thus, K-Number is 3 in this case of Year of Birth of a male being. For females, K-Number is obtained by adding this total to 4. In this case, it is 4+8 = 12 = 1+2 = 3. Interestingly, the K-Number is 3 in this case of Year of Birth of a female being, also. Number 5 is never a K-Number. If 5 is being calculated as the K-Number, then it is straight away taken as, 2 for the males, and 8 for the females.

Personal Year Number concept also exists in the Numerology. Personal Year Number is obtained by the process of addition of current Year number, Mulank and the Number 8, e.g., let the Date of Birth be 22 March 1997, then the Personal Year Number for the current Year 2024 is 2 ((2+0+2+4) + (2+2) + (8) = 20 = 2+0 = 2). Year 2024 for this being is 2nd year. Year 2023, for this being was 1st year. 1st Year means, this being must have had started or done something new in the Year 2023, like, a new business, a foreign visit, purchase of a new car, purchase of a new house, entered into a new important relationship (like marriage) etc.. This being should simply carry forward and keep doing that thing, which he or she had started or done in 1st Year, i.e., Year 2023, in the Year 2024 also, as it is the 2nd Year, now. Number 2 is of the Planet Moon. Moon refers to the Emotions. Emotion is Energy in Motion. Thus, in the Year 2024, this being will be quite emotional, and will have mood swings (sudden or intense changes in the emotional state) as well. For this being, having the Date of Birth as 22

March 1997, in the Year 2025, the Personal Year Number will be 3. Number 3 is of the Planet Jupiter (Guru). Jupiter refers to, teaching, advice, new methods, and eventually the growth.

Name Numerology refers to finding a Name Number, i.e. the numerical value of the Name. The Name Number is also called as the Namank, or the Expression Number. Every Name having a certain Name Number has a certain meaning and a certain frequency. The sound effects of the Name produce certain vibration patterns, meaning and expectations. The Name Number influences areas of being are personal and professional developments. The Name Number determines Whether the Life is Peaceful, successful, or not. The Name Number indicates the kind and the quality, of the other beings, which one attracts and gets associated to in his or her Life. The Name Number indicates the nature of the experiences, which a being will get in his or her Life. The Name Number also indicates the kind of Life one is having, and the Opportunity(s) and Threat(s) in Life. First Name of a being determines the being's Personality. First Name also determines the Desires and the Thought Process. Surname indicates being's Characteristics, and the heredity influence of being's family including those of his or her ancestors. Full Name, i.e. First Name + Surname makes the being's Destiny. Analyses of the numbers of every letter in the Name give the corresponding Expression Number. In the Numerology, an Expression Number or the Name Number represents one's, core, identity, talents and the challenges. Expression Number or the Name Number provides insights into the personal and professional Life, and its analyses tell, How to make the most of one's Strengths. The Personality Number is obtained by looking at only the Consonants in the Name.

The Name Number is obtained as per the Table 1, as given below. This Table 1 is the Pythagorean System or the Western System, one of the many Numerology Systems, for the purpose of allocating the numerical values to the alphabets, in order to obtain the numerical vibrations of the alphabets. Other such Systems are, the Chaldean System, and the Kabbalah System.

Table 1: Pythagorean Numerology

1	2	3	4	5	6	7	8	9
A	B	C	D	E	F	G	H	I
J	K	L	M	N	O	P	Q	R
S	T	U	V	W	X	Y	Z	

Let, the Full Name is Vinit Baba. It decodes to $(4 + 9 + 5 + 9 + 2) + (2 + 1 + 2 + 1) = 35 = 3 + 5 = 8$. Hence, the Name Number of Vinit Baba name is 8.

Exceptions are 11, 22 and 33. 11, 22 and 33 are the Master Numbers. The Master Numbers, which appear in pairs, are more powerful than the other numbers. A beings, which's Name Number is a Master Number, has heightened intuition, potential, and the intelligence.

Mulank, Bhagyank and the Name Number can be different from each other. Mulank can be influenced by free will or the changing the habits or the Name or the Education or the Society. Bad affects of Bhagyank can be mitigated by proper and positive use of Mantra, Tantra, Yantra, Gemstones, or the remedies for the Planets. Birth Number is given importance over the Name Number. Name Number which is matter of one's choice should be in harmony with his or her Birth Number, which is not the matter of one's choice, but the God's will, except for the Birth Numbers 4 and 8. Therefore, Numerological Name Changes are always advised to all beings. Names can be spelt differently by adding extra alphabets to make the Name Number numerologically suitable. Numerological Name Changes are very common among the Celebrities, Movie Names, House Names etc..

In the Astrology, Birth Number, Destiny Number, Zodiac Sign and the Number Numbers are of paramount importance.

Mobile Phone Number Numerology refers to the selection of suitable Mobile Phone Number, which brings good luck, peace and happiness in the Life. A positive Mobile Phone Number brings / increases the positive energy. Mobile Phone Number affects Luck, Communication, Stress and Confidence. Choose a Mobile Phone Number, resonating with the aspirations, by using the Mobile Phone Number Numerology.

Personality Number is also known as the Dream Number or the Inner-Dream Number. The Personality Number is obtained by calculating the Consonants of the Name. The Personality Number reveals one's Personality, and the Persona, i.e. how others perceive you.

Soul Number is also known as the Soul Urge Number or the Heart Desire Number. The Soul Number is obtained by calculating the Vowels of the Name. The Soul Number reveals one's Likes, Dislikes, Inner Strengths and the Resources.

Karmic Numbers are the numbers denoting one's karmic debt(s), which he or she owes, if associated with any of these Karmic Numbers. Karmic Numbers are 13, 14, 16 and 19. Any being born on these dates 13 or 14 or 16 or 19 of any month are born along with a baggage of karmic debts of this Life and the past lives. Have good thoughts, and do good actions, in order to get rid of these karmic debts. Negative Karma can only be balanced out by Positive and Good Karma.

"Purple State Manifestation", greatly helps in the Life. Purple Colour is said to have the maximum energy and the healing properties, among all other known Colours in this Universe. Violet Colour is also very close to the Purple Colour. Violet is a Spectral Colour, and has a relatively shorter wavelength. Purple Colour is a Composite Color, which is made up of Blue Colour and the Red Colour. Manifest a Violet Colour Flame around yourself in order to shed the existing problems of the Life. Similarly, to get the Divine Blessing in the Life, manifest a Purple Colour light descending upon you from the heavens, and entering the body through the Crown Chakra. Manifest bathing in this Purple Colour divine light of the highest and the heightened energy. It is called as the "Purple State Manifestation".

Vehicle's registration number should be compatible with the Date of Birth of its owner. Get the vehicle registration number, whose sum total of last 4 numbers is either number 5 or number 7, e.g. UP 16 AK 9889. It is an Angel Number. Also, its sum total is 7 (9+8+8+9 = 34 = 3+4 = 7). It is very good vehicle registration number. Number 5 and 7 have no enemies. Number 5 is still better over the number 7. Vehicle registration number, whose sum total of last 4 numbers is 1, will be driven more, and will never have natural accident. Number 1 is the number or the Sun. Vehicle registration number, whose sum total of last 4 numbers is 2, will be driven more, without purpose. Number 2 is the number of the Moon. Vehicle registration number, whose sum total of last 4 numbers is 3, will be driven less, and always with purpose. Number 3 is the number of the Jupiter. Vehicle registration number, whose sum total of last 4 numbers is 4, should be driven for commercial purposes, and not for the home or the personal use. Such a vehicle, whose registration number's sum total of last 4 numbers is 4, will be used a lot, brings a lot of money, and has no natural accidents. It is good for trucks, lorries, cabs etc.. Number 4 is the number of the Uranus (Rahu). Vehicle registration number, whose sum total of last 4 numbers is 5, will be used a lot for hill driving. The user of such vehicle, whose registration number's sum total of last 4 numbers is 5, will very frequently take this vehicle for nature excursions, involving, lots of greenery, lake, river, fountains etc.. Number 5 is the number of the Mercury (Buddh). Vehicle registration number, whose sum total of last 4 numbers is 6, will be well-maintained by its owner or the user. Number 6 is the number of the Venus (Shukra). Vehicle registration number, whose sum total of last 4 numbers is 7, will be used for travel to the religious places, and in case, if it goes for the repair and maintenance, then it will remain in the Workshop or the Garage for a longer time, due to one reason or the other, say non-availability of needed part(s). Number 7 is the number of the Neptune (Ketu). Number 7 is a spiritual number. Vehicle registration number, whose sum total of last 4 numbers is 8, should be driven for commercial purposes, especially iron business, and not for the home. Such a vehicle, whose registration number's sum total of last 4 numbers is 8, will be used a lot, brings a lot of money, and has no natural accidents. It is good for trucks, lorries, cabs etc.. Number 8 is the number of the Saturn (Shani). Vehicle registration number, whose sum total of last 4 numbers is 9, will be/should be, of red or rust or orange colour, i.e. the colour of the Mars (the ruling planet of number 9). Vehicle registration number, whose sum total of last 4 numbers is 9, is good for commercial purposes. Vehicle registration number, whose sum total of last 4 numbers is 9, will have frequent breakdowns, often due to the wiring. Number 9 is the number of the Mars (Mangal).

24 Number is the Number of Kuber. Kuber is the God of Wealth, Riches and Treasures. Wear a pendant of 24 Number, if you do not have number 6 is your Date of Birth or the Birth Chart. Wearing a pendant of 24 Number brings the power and the energy of Number 6 and the Planet Venus, into the Life. Number 6 is of Luxury. Presence of Number 6, in the Date of Birth or the Birth Chart, simply means, "more fruits for less efforts".

Beings having 5, 6, and 7 in their Date of Birth (combination of Buddh - Shukra - Ketu), study from abroad, do job abroad, and there is a great likelihood that they will also get settled abroad. Put rotating Globe in the North of the House in order to create the prospects of the foreign visits. Put Mobile Phone Number Wallpaper of the Country, which you wish to visit; Power of Manifestation. What we manifest, we get in the Life.

Use Switchwords and Switchnumbers for intended and faster results of the actions in the Life. Switchwords are the single word affirmations, which have the power to change the Energy. Switchwords influence the Subconscious Mind. Switchwords reprogram the realities of one's Life. Switchwords manifest the Desires. Switchnumbers are the Angel Numbers. Switchnumbers are the special numbers or a repeated appearance of the numbers. Switchnumbers are the Message(s) from the Spiritual Realm. Switchnumbers provide guidance and insight into, Love, Relationships, Marriage, Family, Job, Career, Money, Success and Growth, and other areas of the Life. Repetition of a number increases the significance of the Message. Seeing a number multiple times intensifies the Message(s) from the Spiritual Realm.

"Air Manifestation Technique" also helps in the Life. Inhale till the stomach bloats, and hold it. Then manifest, what you want, as if you already have that thing. Inhaling, then trapping the Breath inside, and not exhaling for some comfortable time, activates the Subconscious Mind. The Subconscious Mind in this state instructs the Conscious Mind to get you all those things, which you had manifested. It is also called as the "Breath Manifestation".

One's Life is affected by the Time, the Space, Situations and the Circumstances, and the Eligibility of that being.

Pygmalion Effect or Rosenthal Effect exists in the Life, provided one is really eligible for it. Universe does it. The Pygmalion Effect is a self-fulfilling prophecy. Pygmalion, a Greek Sculptor, had sculpted a Belle, i.e. a very beautiful woman. Pygmalion's Wish had converted this beautiful sculpted woman sculpture into a living woman, and he married her then. Pygmalion Effect or Rosenthal Effect occurs, when High Expectations lead to the improved performance. Remember, Low Expectations worsen the performance.

Very frequently, use Psychic Surgery, Stones, Colours, Symbols and the Crystals for improving the self-energies and levels of the self-consciousness, for the purpose of an accomplished Life. Becoming Zero (the Shiva), at the end, is the final aim of the Life. Also, use the Affirmations in the Life, on a very regular basis, "I am too blessed", "I am the happiest being", "Thank you God for the everything, you have given to me, in my Life", "I am the super rich being", "I am very successful", "I am the peaceful soul", "I am the strongest soul", "I am very handsome (or beautiful)" etc.. Universe listens everything, respects our intentions, and then fulfills it; the Law of Attraction. What is not available is being made available, by the Universe; it is the secret Power of the Affirmations.

Do not take any loan on the Tuesday and the Saturday, as it will make its payment very difficult. Wednesday and Friday are recommended days for getting a loan, say, a house loan, or a study loan, or a vehicle loan. Make payments of salary, loan etc., on Saturday only. Workers, Labourers, Helps and Maids represent Saturn, therefore, keep them very happy, often give them sweets, talk to them with respect and gently, and be decent to them. Saturn is the Planet of Success and the Achievements, but slow, and also, along with a bit of struggles. Saturn is the Planet of Poetic Justice.

There are subtle energy channels in the Human Body, also known as the Nadi (नाड़ी). When we breathe through the left nostril, it is the Ida Nadi or the Chandra Nadi. In Sanskrit language, the word, "Ida" means "comfort". Ida Nadi is connected to the Moon. Moon represents cold. Ida Nadi is associated with the feminine energy. Ida Nadi is an energy channel, which is associated with the left side of the Body, and the right hemisphere of the Brain. When we breathe through the right nostril, it is the Pingala Nadi or the Surya Nadi. Pingala Nadi is connected to the Sun. Sun represents hot. Pingala Nadi is associated with the masculine energy. Pingala Nadi is an energy channel, which is associated with the right side of the Body, and the left hemisphere of the Brain. Most of the time, beings breath-in, through any one nostril only. In the state of the transition, from Ida to Pingala, or from Pingala to Ida, for four minutes, we breathe through both the nostrils, and in this state, Sushumna Nadi is active. In Sanskrit language, Sushumna Nadi means the central energy channel. Sushumna Nadi runs through the Spine. Sushumna Nadi is the most important Nadi. Sushumna Nadi is the key channel for the flow of Shakti Energy. These are the secrets of Yoga for the daily Life. Do Yoga regularly for a healthy and a happy Life. Meditation and Yoga improve Sympathetic Nervous System (SNS) within the Body. SNS is that part of the Nervous System of the Body, which prepares the Body to respond to stressful or emergent situations. SNS is also known as the "Fight-or-Flight" Mechanism of the Body.

In the Vedic Astrology, Pitra Dosh or Pitru Dosha (पितृ दोष) refers to the negative Karmic Debt(s) of the ancestors. Dosha means fault or weakness or shortcoming. Pitru Dosha is any wrongdoing committed by an individual against their parents. Pitru Dosha brings obstacles and troubles in the lives of the descendants. Pitru Dosha is the presence of unsettled ancestral spirits. Pitru Dosha is caused by unresolved ancestral Karma. Pitru Dosha leads to normal health problems, mental health problems, family conflicts, career problems, financial constraints etc.. Pitru Dosha occurs, when in the Birth Chart or the Horoscope, Sun and Moon are placed in the 9th House of the Horoscope, or Saturn is placed in the 9th House of the Horoscope, or Rahu is placed in the 9th House of the Horoscope, or Ketu is placed in the 4th House of the Horoscope. Pitru Dosha is addressed by performing the Shradha rituals, Charity, and certain spiritual practices during Pitru Paksha (the fortnight of the paternal ancestors). Wearing a Ruby gemstone also helps in eliminating ill effects of Pitru Dosha in one's Life. Pitru

Dosha is same as the Kaal Sarp Dosha. Kaal Sarp Dosha is an astrological alignment, where all seven planets are between the Rahu and the Ketu in one's Birth Chart or the Horoscope. Kaal Sarp Dosha is one of the most serious and concerning Doshas in the Horoscope. Pitru Dosha or Kaal Sarp Dosh is basically the Rahu Dosha. Rahu Dosha means that Rahu is negative. Do prescribed remedies for Rahu for Pitru Dosha or Kaal Sarp Dosha or Rahu Dosha removal from the Life.

Happiness is one of the purposes of the Life, Peace is another. Happiness is brought about by 4 hormones, i.e. 4 chemical elements, which are released in the Body. These chemicals, when released, create a chemical high in the Body and of the state of the Mind. These 4 chemical elements are Dopamine, Oxytocin, Serotonin and Endorphin. Dopamine is the hormone of Rewards and Achievements. Dopamine is a Neurotransmitter. Dopamine plays an important role in 3 Ms, i.e. 3 Body functions viz. the Memory, the Movement and the Motivation. Dopamine affects mental health and neurological state of the Body. Oxytocin is the hormone of Love and the Relationships. Oxytocin is released by expressing gratitude, and by exercising the habit of giving, i.e. by becoming a Giver. Oxytocin hormone manages female and male reproductive systems, and the aspect like Labor, Delivery and Lactation. Hypothalamus makes the Oxytocin. Hypothalamus is an area of the Brain, which produces Oxytocin hormone, which controls the Body Temperature, Heart Rate and the Hunger. Posterior Pituitary Gland stores the Oxytocin and releases it into the Bloodstream. Serotonin is the hormone of Peace, Calmness and Satisfaction. Serotonin carries messages between the Nerve Cells in the Brain, and also, throughout the Body. Serotonin affects the Mood, the

Sleep, Nausea (a feeling of sickness or discomfort in the Stomach, often associated with an urge to Vomit), Digestion, Wound Healing, Blood Clotting, Bone Health, and the Sex Urges & Desires. Endorphin is the hormone released by the physical exercises. Endorphins are released when Body feels Pain and Stress. Endorphins are also produced in the Brain. Endorphins act as the Messengers within the Body.

Do not criticise, the Universe, or the God, or the Life, for the things, which are not there in the Life, but always say Thanks to, the Universe, or the God, or the Life, for all the things, you already have in the Life. Being "Thankful", is the biggest Mantra, for the Happiness, the Success, and the Prosperity, in the Life. Be open, and do not get fixated to any one thing in the Life. Saying "Thanks", with purity, full Faith, full Belief, complete Love and Devotion, to the Universe, or the God, or the Life, will solve/remove the problems of the Life. Do not become selfish, by asking for the self, but ask for the others, associated with you, and thus, you will automatically get, the thing(s), since you are one amongst them. Things will happen in the Life, either good or bad. Domino Effect exists in the Life. No being can stop the occurrence of things; however, we all can definitely control our reactions, and thus, prevent turning the things into their worst states. Beings will hate, rate and shake, but stand and stay strong. A positive reaction is a necessary condition for a happy Life. Very little is needed to make a happy Life, as it is all within the self, i.e. in the way of thinking. Harder times of the Life, help realising the true colours of beings, which are present in his or her Life. A beautiful butterfly undergoes many changes before becoming so beautiful; it is the Life. Change, Adaptation and right Adoption are necessary in the Life.

We learn nothing from the Life, if we keep thinking all the time that we are right. Let bygones be bygones. Be a naiveté. We cannot ride two horses at the same time. Our attitude is, what we are today at this moment. Do not become persona non grata. Don't put all your eggs in one basket. For the ordinary beings, Life seems to be higgledy-piggledy and topsy-turvy. Be equal with all. Any destination can be reached with Inspiration, Liberation and Determination. Forgetting the bad, and forgiving the bad, are the best self-prescribed remedies, as it breaks the vicious cycle of Karma or the Loop of Karma. Only the wearer knows, where the shoe bites. Dharma originates in the logical Mind. If corrections are not being applied by the being in his or her Life, then the Life sua sponte does it, i.e. suo motu. In the Show and the Game of the Life, 04 Factors affect us all through the Life, viz. Time, Space or the Place, Situations or the Circumstances, and the Eligibility (whether we are fit to receive grace of the God or something, or not). Be a goody-goody. Is there a persistent feeling of being pipped at the post in various walks of the Life? Go not get upset about all the hoopla surrounding the events of Life. Win by being Different, if not possible to become Better. Life is always very smooth and better, in every sense, ergo, there is no need to score off each other. The journey of the Life is an integration of the watershed moments, i.e. the Dots, making the Line, called the Life. Happiness is the spiritual experience of living every moment of the Life, in full Grace, and with extremeum Love and deep Gratitude. Do Meditation regularly, and make the Hope, a much stronger emotion over the Fear. Meditation is not godforsaken. We are gobsmacked, when finding out the benefits of Meditation; do not be cagey, telling its benefits to others. Peace and

Happiness in the Life, i.e. the D-Day is brought into the Life through the instrumentality of Prayer, Yoga, Meditation and the Spiritual Practices (the Spirituality). Have a go-to Preceptor. Enlightenment happens on a slow burn. Experience means Mistakes; but take one from one made, one of its kinds, only once. Life is a cornucopia in its all aspects. Life is not for the mundane, but for the magun opus. Do not add Years to the Life, but add the life to the Years of the Life. Meditation does the Mind Management, shuffle off the problems, and converts the Pressures of the Life, into the Pleasures of the Life. Be a bit feisty. Do not indulge in grandstanding, be humble, and do not call the shots. Do not hang in the balance. Have the spunk. Life is kinda a game; play it well, and become a mesomorph Wunderkind. Have the Life's motto "Carpe diem," and carefully contrive to live down to it; we all are Habitué of this Earth, other Earths, and the other Planets in this infinite Cosmos. Train the Mind and the Heart to see the good, in everything. What we do, when we do not get the success, decides the forthcoming success. Universe gives prescient instructions, Advice, and also, Warnings. Become spiritually rich in your own right. In the Journey of Life, keep doing the little things for the Others, as these little things done, make a big place in the hearts, over a period of time. Life is an agreement between the two, scilicet, the being and the universe. God has a definite plan for every being, i.e. the best plan. Nature turns the tables for each one of us. Performativity exists in the Life. We all are essentially the Spiritual Beings, and not the Human Beings, with certain Human-Life Journey Experiences. We all are Vibrations. We all are Energies. Practise Kinaesthetic Learning through Yoga. Add, the Colours, and the Values, to the Life.

This Book on Numerology, holding and containing within, the World of Numbers, is perfectly fitting in your hands; dang, not knowing it.

CHAPTER TWO

Mulank 1

Beings, which are born on 1, 10, 19 or 28 of any month, have Mulank 1. Mulank 1 or the Number 1 is ruled and influenced by the planet Sun or the Surya. Sun refers to, "I am". Sun represents Creative Energies, i.e. Nature of the Self, the Life Purpose and the Consciousness. Mulank 1 represents the Self. Sun is the King, and also, a fatherly figure. Sun is Real and Honest and Ambitious. Sun symbolises Pride and the Image. It is believed that the Sun is also cruel at times.

Characteristics - Strengths and Weaknesses of Beings born with Mulank 1 are as follows:

Strengths:

Beings with Mulank 1 are quite Powerful, Masculine and the born Leaders. Beings with Mulank 1 are very Original and Right, Honest and True, Helping, Hardworking, Dominating, Independent, Risk-taking, Decisive, Efficient, Strong, Matured, Courageous, Authoritative, Lucky, Self-aware, and quite Self-confident. Beings having Mulank 1 are Givers. Beings with Mulank 1 are Aggressive and Creative in their Nature. Beings with Mulank 1 possess good controlling abilities. Beings with Mulank 1 maintain good bonds with other beings. Beings, born with Mulank 1, make matured and good decisions in their Life. Beings with

Mulank 1 always stay positively reinforced. Beings with Mulank 1 are Image-conscious. Beings with Mulank 1 are Freedom Lovers.

Weaknesses:

Strengths of beings are also their Weaknesses. Beings with Mulank 1 are Bossy, Aggressive, Egoistic and Stubborn, and sometimes Selfish and Cruel. Beings with Mulank 1 are Workaholic; such beings may not have much time for the others. Beings with Mulank 1 are not lucky in love matters, which need time.

Friend-Number(s):

Planets, Moon, Mars, Jupiter, Neptune and the Uranus, are friendly Planets of the Sun. Beings, which are ruled by these Planets, viz. Moon, Mars, Jupiter, Neptune and the Uranus remain in harmony with Mulank 1 beings. Thus, for beings having Mulank 1, beings having Mulank 2, 9, 3, 5, 7, and 4 are friends. Mulank 2, 9, 3, 5, 7, and 4 are Firend-Numbers or Compatible Numbers of Mulank 1.

Anti-Number(s) and Remedies:

Planets, Venus and Saturn are enemy Planets of the Sun. Therefore, beings with Mulank or Numbers 6 and 8, are not friendly for beings having Mulank 1. Mulanks 6 and 8 are the Anti-Numbers or the Non - Compatible Numbers of Mulank 1. Interestingly, it has also been observed that whenever Being with Mulank 1 comes in association with other being with Mulank 4, there are chances that, Being with Mulank 1 may suffer injuries, or may have health related issues or problems, or even may get landed in some other troubles or controversies.

Akashic Records give Remedies to the problems of the Life, which are created on the account of bad Karma of present Life and of the past Life(s). Simplest Remedy is Forgiveness for mistakes of the others. Penance and

Positive Karma are the best remedies for the mistakes done by the self. Meditation reveals, the Secrets of the Life, and of the Universe. Manifestation is the best Remedy. Changing the Mindset and Lifestyle are also good remedies.

Remedy(s) is/are to be done, for the Anti-Number(s), by pleasing these Anti-Number(s) associated Planet(s), as mentioned in the Chapter 1, or by pleasing the gods associated with these Planets by regular prayers, chanting and worshipping, or regular offerings to these Planets or the gods, or doing the right rituals everyday or right day(s), in order to placate them (associated Planets, associated gods), and make them happy.

Remedies:

Make Fire element strong. Have Kitchen, or put a Fire Painting or a Flame or Electrical Gadget(s) in the South-East (SE) Direction of the House or the Home, as per the Vaastu.

Best Career/Profession:

For Beings with Mulank 1, best Career or Profession are Hotel, Cafeteria, Restaurants, Electrical & Electronics, Entrepreneurship, Heads of Organisations, Defense Forces, Bureaucracy, Politics and International Affairs.

Lucky Day:

Lucky Day for Beings having Mulank 1 is Sunday. Plan and do all major and important activities on Sunday only. 19 and 28 dates of the Month are the luckiest dates for beings having Mulank 1. Lucky Days are the favourable days, special days, best days, more beneficial, give additional strength, and bring good news to the beings.

Lucky Month(s) of Years and Lucky Years of Life:

For Beings having Mulank 1, 1st Month January and 10th Month October are the Lucky Months. Lucky Years of the Life for Beings having Mulank 1 are 1st year, 10th year, 19th year, 28th year, 37th year, 46th year, 55th year, 64th year, 73rd year, 82nd year, 91st year and the 100th year. Lucky Months and Lucky Years are the favourable months and the years, and bring good news (unexpected financial gains, growth, job, promotion, marriage, children etc.) to the beings.

Lucky Colours:

Lucky Colours for Beings having Mulank 1 are Red and Orange. These are the Colours of Sun. Beings with Mulank 1 should wear, and keep the things (like Clothing, Pillows and Cushions Covers, Curtains, Drapery, Tablecloths, Bed sheets etc.) only with these Colours with themselves, and try remaining in the surroundings of these Colours only.

Our Nature is our Future. We all should try to become Poetry in Motion. Be Conscious and Awakened, and thus, stop yourself from Descending into the Rabbit Hole. Stuff yourself to the Gunwales with the Spiritual Elements. Manage the Mind. Mind does not differentiate between the Imagination and the Reality. Use the Powers of the Subconscious Mind, the Power of Now, the Power of Affirmations, and the Law of Attraction, in the Life. Do Deep Breathing, and practise the Mindfulness, for the Best Life.

Mulank 2

Beings, which are born on 2, 11, 20 or 29 of any month, have Mulank 2. Mulank 2 or the Number 2 is ruled and influenced by the planet Moon or the Chandrama. Number 2 is a good number. Moon refers to, "I feel". Moon represents the Inner Being, i.e. Feelings, Reaction and the Soul Development. Mulank 2 represents the Femininity or the Womanliness. Moon represents Class, Sensitivity and Emotions. Beings having Mulank 2 are quite traditional, and family - oriented.

Characteristics - Strengths and Weaknesses of Beings born with Mulank 2 are as follows:

Strengths:

Beings with Mulank 2 are ever-changing and nature lovers. Beings with Mulank 2 are good Guides and Healers, and are good in supportive roles. Beings with Mulank 2 possess good imaginative power. Beings having Mulank 2 are very kind-hearted, suave & naïve, sincere, faithful towards their duties, helpful, caring, subtle, gentle and peaceful. Beings with Mulank 2 wish to live in harmony, and are ardent music lovers. Beings having Mulank 2 have good sense of humour. Being with Mulank 2, respect others, accept their viewpoints, and also, accept the proposal of others. Being having Mulank 2 are very good planners.

Weaknesses:

Strengths of beings are also beings weaknesses. Beings with Mulank 2 get excited quite easily. Beings having Mulank 2 are inconsistent and lack continuity. Women having Mulank 2 feel more emotional ups and downs as compared to the Men having Mulank 2. Beings having Mulank 2 cannot say No to others for anything; as a result, many times they land up in some problem or trouble. Beings having Mulank 2 are lazy. Beings with Mulank 2 are quite sentimental. Beings having Mulank 2 have mood swings. Beings with Mulank 2 can easily go into depression, and may even develop suicidal tendencies.These beings have too many ups and downs in the Life, and worry a lot.

Friend-Number(s):

Sun, Jupiter, Uranus, Neptune, Saturn, and the Mars, are friendly planets of the Moon. Beings, which are ruled by these Planets, viz. Sun, Jupiter, Uranus, Neptune, Saturn, and the Mars, remain in harmony with Mulank 2 beings. Thus, for beings having Mulank 2, beings having Mulanks 1, 3, 4, 7, 8 and 9 are friends. Mulanks 1, 3, 4, 7, 8 and 9 are Friend - Numbers or Compatible Numbers of Mulank 2.

Anti-Number(s) and Remedies:

Mercury and Venus are unfriendly to the Moon. Therefore, beings with Mulank or Numbers 5 and 6 are not friendly for beings having Mulank 2. Mulanks 5 and 6 are Anti - Numbers or Non-Compatible Numbers of Mulank 2.

Akashic Records give Remedies to the Problems of Life, created on the account of bad Karma of present Life and the past lives. Simplest Remedy is Forgiveness for mistakes. Meditation reveals, the Secrets of the Life, and of the Universe. Manifestation is the best Remedy. Changing the Mindset and Lifestyle are also very good Remedies.

Remedy(s) is/are to be done, for the Anti-Number(s), by pleasing these Anti-Number(s) associated Planet(s), as mentioned in the Chapter 1, or by pleasing the gods associated with these Planets by regular prayers, chanting and worshipping, or regular offerings to these Planets or the gods, or doing the right rituals everyday or right day(s), in order to placate them (associated Planets, associated gods), and make them happy.

Remedies:

Make Water element strong. Have Water Taps, Hand-pump, Well(if), Swimming Pool, or put a Spring or Waterfall or Sea or River Painting or an Aquarium in the North-East (NE) Direction of the House or the Home, as per the Vaastu.

Best Career/Profession:

For Beings with Mulank 2, best Career or Profession are Singing, Fine Arts, Imaginative and Creative Arts, Designing, Theatre, Animation, Hotel Industry, Food and Catering, Grocery Stores, Milk Business, Dairy, Chocolates, Health Care and Hospitals, and Software and Information Technology.

Lucky Day:

Lucky Day for Beings having Mulank 2 is Monday. Plan and perform various activities on Monday. Mondays falling on 1, 4, 7, 10, 13, 16, 19, 22, 25, 28, 31 dates of the Month are the luckiest dates. Lucky Days are the favourable days, special days, best days, more beneficial, give additional strength, and bring good news to the beings.

Lucky Month(s) of Years and Lucky Years of Life:

For Beings having Mulank 2, 2nd Month February, and 11th Month November, are the Lucky Months of the year. Lucky Years of the Life for Beings having Mulank 2 are 2nd year, 11th year, 20th year, 29th year, 38th year, 47th year,

56th year, 65th year, 74th year, 83rd year and the 92nd year. Any other year of the life, which is divisible by Number 2 will also be beneficial. Lucky Months and Lucky Years are the favourable months and the years, and bring good news (unexpected financial gains, growth, job, promotion, marriage, children etc.) to the beings.

Lucky Colour:

Lucky Colour for Beings having Mulank 2 is White. Moon is of White Colour. Beings with Mulank 2 should wear, and keep the things (like Clothing, Pillows and Cushions Covers, Curtains, Drapery, Tablecloths, Bed Sheets etc.) of White Colour with themselves, and try remaining in the surrounding of this White Colour. Light Green Colour is also recommended for Beings having Mulank 2, as it is better for their mental health, mental power and nervous system.

Silence has always a lot to tell, but we fail to get it. Do not be insular. Present time of the life is off the back of the past time, choices made and the decisions taken. Chart a new and a better path in the life. Turn the Nelson's eye to the bad and the unpleasant. Do not follow suit. Avoid facing the dilemma arising due to the thoughts overkill. Try to be in a good company always, if do not want to stay alone. Change yourself. Change is the Law of Nature. A butterfly, before becoming beautiful, undergoes lots of pains, and the states of change. Love, and respect all. Listen full, understand full, think right and less, and do not react, but respond. One's life is at its best, when he or she becomes the reason(s) of other's happiness. Stay cheerful. Never get drowned in a sea of schmaltz. Goal of the Life is very simple; become better than yesterday. Always commiserate with weak beings. Burst in with the wise beings hot on their heels; do not fail to fall back upon such beings. Weigh in with your suggestions in all situations and circumstances of the Life. Try pulling off a brilliant every time by pushing the envelope, i.e. draw the first blood. With the proper mind control, rule the roost. Do not get involved in any machination. Do not limit your challenges, but challenge your limits. The journey of life in the physical form is too short. Remember, Pain is the price for Pleasure. Become a lighthouse through spiritual evolution. Work on Body, Mind and the Spirit or the Soul. We all, are here for a Reason, a very good and a very great Reason. We all, have a specific Purpose of Life. This prized Life should be a tour de force.

CHAPTER FOUR

Mulank 3

Beings, which are born on 3, 12, 21 or 30 of any month, have Mulank 3. Mulank 3 or the Number 3 is ruled and influenced by the Guru or the planet Jupiter. Number 3 is a good number. Jupiter refers to, "I teach". Jupiter represents Expansion, i.e. Spirit, Assimilation and Compensation. Jupiter is the planet of Wisdom and Knowledge. Guru or Jupiter is nonchalant in its nature. Jupiter is the Mentor, and a Giver. Jupiter is a Spiritual Planet. Jupiter is the Master Planet, and not the jack of all trades. Beings having Mulank 3 are remembered by their future generations. Beings having Mulank 3 are very Visionary and quite inspiring.

Characteristics - Strengths and Weaknesses of Beings born with Mulank 3 are as follows:

Strengths:

Beings with Mulank 3 are honest, kind, loving, caring, creative, ambitious and disciplined. Beings having Mulank 3 are healthy, and full of stamina and endurance, with a strong well-built body. Beings with Mulank 3 are quite professional and very hard working, and have a very successful career and achieve greater heights in their Life. Beings having Mulank 3 are successful entrepreneurs and the business owners. Beings having Mulank 3 possess effective communication skills. Beings having Mulank 3 are job givers, and not the job seekers. Beings having Mulank 3 are very good guides, mentors, motivators, advisors, teachers and the leaders. Beings having Mulank 3 are family-oriented, and also, take a keen interest in the social works.

Weaknesses:

Strengths of beings are also beings weaknesses. Strengths of beings are also beings weaknesses. Beings with Mulank 3 are impulsive, sensitive to criticism, non-punctual, disapproving of their looks, irresponsible, indecisive and full of arrogance.

Friend-Number(s):

Sun, Moon, Mercury, Venus, Saturn, and the Mars are the friendly planets of the Jupiter. Beings, which are ruled by these Planets, viz. Sun, Moon, Mercury, Venus, Saturn, and the Mars, remain in harmony with Mulank 3 beings. Thus, for beings having Mulank 3, beings having Mulanks 1, 2, 5, 8 and 9 are friends. Mulanks 1, 2, 5, 6, 8 and 9 are Friend-Numbers or Compatible Numbers of Mulank 3.

Anti-Number(s) and Remedies:

Uranus and Neptune are unfriendly to the Jupiter. Therefore, beings with Mulank or Numbers 4, 6 and 7 are not friendly for beings having Mulank 3. Mulanks 4, 6 and 7 are Anti-Numbers or Non-Compatible Numbers of Mulank 3. Combination 36 is very bad (36 का आंकड़ा).

Akashic Records give Remedies to the Problems of Life, which are created on the account of bad Karma of present Life and the past lives. Simplest Remedy is Forgiveness for mistakes. Meditation reveals, the Secrets of the Life, and of the Universe. Manifestation is the best Remedy. Changing the Mindset and Lifestyle are also very good Remedies.

Remedy(s) is/are to be done, for the Anti-Number(s), by pleasing these Anti-Number(s) associated Planet(s), as mentioned in the Chapter 1, or by pleasing the gods associated with these Planets by regular prayers, chanting and worshipping, or regular offerings to these Planets or the gods, or doing the right rituals everyday or right day(s), in order to placate them (associated Planets, associated gods), and make them happy.

Remedies:

Make Sky or Ether or Space element strong. Sky or the Akaash (आकाश) is never ending. Space is full of constellations. Sky contains the galaxies, Sun, Moon, Planets, and Stars. Space is the Universe, i.e. "the Brahamaand". Sky is the place of the God. Space has lots of importance in our lives. There is a Space outside, and another Space inside. Vaastu gives different directions for better Spaces. Have an Open Space in the Centre of the home or the house. Akaash is a Brahmasthan, which should always be an open place in the Centre of the home or the house.

Best Career/Profession:

For Beings having Mulank 3, best Career or Profession are Professor, Tutor, College Owner, School Owner, Coaching Institutes, Singing, Music Composing, Fine Arts, Imaginative and Creative Arts, Designing, Theatre, Banking, Chartered Accountancy, Interior Designing, Architecture and Planning, Real Estate and Property Dealing, Construction and Civil Engineering.

Lucky Day:

Lucky Day for Beings having Mulank 3 is Thursday. Plan and do the activities on Thursday. Thursdays falling on 1, 2, 3, 5, 6, 8, 9, 10, 11, 12, 14, 15, 17, 18, 19, 20, 21, 23, 24, 26,

27, 28, 29, and 30 dates of the Month are the luckiest dates. Lucky Days are the favourable days, special days, best days, more beneficial, give additional strength, and bring good news to the beings.

Lucky Month(s) of Years and Lucky Years of Life:

For Beings having Mulank 3, 3rd Month March and 12th Month December are the Lucky Months. Lucky Years of the Life for Beings having Mulank 3 are 3rd year, 12th year, 21st year, 30th year, 39th year, 48th year, 57th year, 66th year, and the 75th year. Any other year of the life, which is divisible by Number 3 will also be beneficial. Lucky Months and Lucky Years are the favourable months and the years, and bring good news (unexpected financial gains, growth, job, promotion, marriage, children etc.) to the beings.

Lucky Colours:

Lucky Colours for Beings having Mulank 3 are Yellow and Blue. Beings with Mulank 3 should wear, and keep the things (like Clothing, Pillows and Cushions Covers, Curtains, Drapery, Tablecloths, Bedsheets etc.) with Yellow and Blue Colours with themselves, and try remaining in the surroundings of these Yellow and Blue Colours. Beings having Mulank 3 should avoid things of Red and Black Colours.

Discipline is the Destiny. The Mantra to Win, and to get Success is, "it is Never Over, till actually it is Over, and it is Never". Time is the Dot. Life is the Line. Line is a slide of the Dot. Expectations from the self are always inspirational, while expectations from others may prove to be hurtful at times. We have experiences of the Life, but that's about it. Life, and every moment of its Journey, is a Clean Slate. Every Journey of Life is a port of call. Life is, not happening to us, but for us. We are the Souls, filled with Peace & Joy, and Compassion & Kindness. Grief is the part of the Life's Design for all. Just when you think, things are working out well; the Life will throw a curveball. 05 Stages for overcoming any Grief in the Life are Denial, Anger, Depression, Negotiation, and the Acceptance. Feel the Feelings. Purpose of Grief, is to take us, to the higher Levels of Awareness and Spiritual Awakening. Internalise the values of Honesty and Perseverance. Do not rock the boat. In our Life, we are the Product of our own Definitions and Decisions.

CHAPTER FIVE

Mulank 4

Beings, which are born on 4, 13, 22 or 31 of any month, have Mulank 4. Mulank 4 or the Number 4 is ruled and influenced by the Yama and/or Arun (or Rahu), or the planets Pluto and/or the Uranus, respectively. Rahu is North node of the Moon. Rahu is not a real Planet. Rahu is a pseudo Planet. Rahu is a shadow Planet. Rahu has Head, but no remaining Body. Pluto is a dwarf Planet. Pluto has not cleared its neighboring region of other objects. Uranus is an ice giant. Uranus doesn't have a true surface. The Planet Uranus is mostly swirling fluids. Uranus comes within a minimum of about 11 Astronomical Unit (AU) from Pluto. 1 AU is 1.496e+8 Kilometres. Number 4 is not a good number. Number 4 stands for Secrecy. Pluto refers to, "I desire". Pluto represents Transition, i.e. Life - Death - Rebirth, Cycles, Power Sources and Compulsions. Rahu is Practical and Unorthodox. Rahu is Secretive, Disobedient, Rebel and Non-conformist (परंपरा-विरोधी). Beings having Mulank 4 do not, run with the herd and swim with the tide, but against all these. Beings having Mulank 4 add Perspectives (thoughts) so as to create the newer Realities. Beings having Mulank 4 have to do a lot of hard work in their Life. Beings having Mulank 4 have a big Heart, who easily give Money, and other kind of help to others, even when, they don't have much Money and other Resources. Even, Mulank 4 beings borrow the Money from the others to give it to the needy. Females born on 4, 13, 22 and 31, after their Marriage, are very lucky for their Husbands and In-laws, specially in terms of Money, Wealth and overall Prosperity. These Females become Lucky for the self also, only after the Marriage, and are Lucky Lady (सौभाग्यवती).

Characteristics - Strengths and Weaknesses of Beings born with Mulank 4 are as follows:

Strengths:

Beings with Mulank 4 are Bold, Logical, Affectionate, Disciplined, quite rigid in their Attitude, and least Tolerant. Beings having Mulank 4 have leadership qualities and good convincing power, and rule over the others. Beings having Mulank 4 are out of the box Thinkers. Beings having Mulank 4 oppose the things and have a rebellion Nature. Beings having Mulank 4, are quite neat and tidy, and carry good personality. Beings having Mulank 4 are influential Speakers with sharp Intellect and good Memory. Beings having Mulank 4 are Creative and Mystical. Beings having Mulank 4 love Music & Dance. Beings having Mulank 4 are Critics. Beings having Mulank 4 are Learners, Punctual, Scrupulous, Consistent, Methodical, Meticulous and Fastidious. Beings with Mulank 4 are very Generous and Helpful. Beings having Mulank 4 are Givers, and cannot say "No" to anybody. Beings with Mulank 4 have to face continuous struggles in their Life.

Weaknesses:

Strengths of beings are also beings weaknesses. Beings having Mulank 4 get attracted to beings having Anti–Numbers of Mulank 4, viz. 3 and 8. Beings having

Mulank 4 are Rigid, Short-tempered, Abrupt, Critical, Stubborn, Risk-aversive, Intolerant, and Egoist & Egotist.

Friend-Number(s):

Sun, Moon, Mercury, Venus, Neptune and Mars are the friendly Planets of the Uranus. Beings, which are ruled by these Planets, viz. Sun, Moon, Mercury, Venus, Neptune and the Mars, remain in harmony with Mulank 4 beings. Thus, for beings having Mulank 4, beings having Mulanks 1, 2, 5, 6, 7 and 9 are Friends. Mulanks 1, 2, 5, 6, 7 and 9 are Friend-Numbers or Compatible Numbers of Mulank 4.

Anti-Number(s) and Remedies:

Jupiter and Saturn are unfriendly to Uranus. Therefore, beings with Mulank or Numbers 3 and 8 are not friendly for beings having Mulank 4. Mulanks 3 and 8 are Anti-Numbers or Non-compatible Numbers of Mulank 4.

Akashic Records give Remedies to the Problems of Life, which are created on the account of bad Karma of present Life and the past lives. Simplest Remedy is Forgiveness for mistakes. Meditation reveals, the Secrets of the Life, and of the Universe. Manifestation is the best Remedy. Changing the Mindset and Lifestyle are also very good Remedies.

Remedy(s) is/are to be done, for the Anti-Number(s), by pleasing these Anti-Number(s) associated Planet(s), as mentioned in the Chapter 1, or by pleasing the gods associated with these Planets by regular prayers, chanting and worshipping, or regular offerings to these Planets or the gods, or doing the right rituals everyday or right day(s), in order to placate them (associated Planets, associated gods), and make them happy.

Remedies:

Make Fire element strong. Have Kitchen, or put a Fire Painting or a Flame or Electrical Gadget(s) in the South-East (SE) Direction of the House or the Home, as per the

Vaastu.

Best Career/Profession:

For Beings having Mulank 4, best Career or Profession are Computer Business, IT Sector, Real Estate, Transport Business, Banking and InfoTech Business. Any career or business involving creativity is also good for the beings having Mulank 4.

Lucky Day:

Lucky Day for Beings having Mulank 4 is Sunday. Plan and do activities on Sunday. Sundays falling on 4 or 13 or 22 or 31 dates of the Month are the luckiest dates. Lucky Days are the favourable days, special days, best days, more beneficial, give additional strength, and bring good news to the beings.

Lucky Month(s) of Years and Lucky Years of Life:

For Beings having Mulank 4, 4th Month April is the Lucky Month. Lucky Years of the Life for Beings having Mulank 4 are 4th year, 13th year, 22nd year, 31st year, 40th year, 49th year, 58th year, 67th year, 76th year and the 85th year. These years are beneficial to beings having Mulank 4, in terms of unexpected gains, jobs, promotions, children and family, marriages etc.. Any other year of the life, which is divisible by Number 4 will also be beneficial. Lucky Months and Lucky Years are the favourable months and the years, and bring good news (unexpected financial gains, growth, job, promotion, marriage, children etc.) to the beings.

Lucky Colours:

Lucky Colour for Beings having Mulank 4 is Grey. Beings with Mulank 4 should wear, and keep the things (like Clothing, Pillows and Cushions Covers, Curtains, Drapery, Tablecloths, Bed sheets etc.) with Grey Colour with themselves, and try remaining in the surroundings of this Grey Colour or the similar shades of Grey Colour.

All of us are sailing in the broken boats. Richness is, neither in earning, nor in spending, but, the richness is in needing "no more". Prayer acts as the bridge between panic and peace. Always be very careful about, what you ask for, from the Universe, as the Universe makes a Conspiracy, and then starts working, so as to give you, what you asked for. Ask the God for three things, viz. Love, Health and the Happiness. What comes, i.e. the Present, is always better than, what has gone away, i.e. the Past. Keep hope alive always, as the good things always happen, when you expect least. In the Life, everything is Destiny, and nothing Coincidence.

CHAPTER SIX

Mulank 5

Beings, which are born on 5, 14, or 23 of any month, have Mulank 5. Mulank 5 or the Number 5 is ruled and influenced by the Buddh or the planet Mercury. Number 5 is a good number. Number 5 is a Psychic Number. Psychic refers to Mind's unusual powers of, seeing into the future, or knowing what somebody else is thinking. Mercury refers to, "I talk". Mercury represents Mentality, i.e. Mind, Communication, Nerves and Senses. Mercury is the Planet of Communication and Entertainment. Beings having Mulank 5 are excellent Communicator, Intelligent and Entertainers, i.e. possess the ability to convert the Boredom into the Fun or into the Recreation.

Characteristics - Strengths and Weaknesses of Beings born with Mulank 5 are as follows:

Strengths:

Beings with Mulank 5 are quite Lucky beings. Beings having Mulank 5 are Visionary, Courageous, Doers, Givers, effective Communicators, good Thinkers, and good Planners. Beings with Mulank 5 are quick Decision Makers.

Weaknesses:

Strengths of beings are also beings Weaknesses. Beings having Mulank 5 get bored very easily. Beings having Mulank 5 are prone to distraction(s), and have difficulty in focussing, i.e. they are vey fidgety. Beings having Mulank 5 are Impatient, Overconfident, Trend-followers, Talkative and Inaccurate. Beings having Mulank 5 have health related issues and problems.

Friend-Number(s):

Sun, Jupiter, Uranus, Venus, Neptune, Saturn, and the Mars are the friendly Planets of the Mercury. Beings, which are ruled by these Planets, viz. Sun, Jupiter, Uranus, Venus, Neptune, Saturn, and the Mars, remain in harmony with Mulank 5 beings. Thus, for beings having Mulank 5, beings having Mulanks 1, 3, 4, 7, 8 and 9 are friends. Mulanks 1, 3, 4, 5, 6, 7, 8 and 9 are Friend-Numbers or Compatible Numbers of Mulank 5.

Anti-Number(s) and Remedies:

Moon is unfriendly to the Mercury. Therefore, beings with Mulank or Number 2 are not friendly for beings having Mulank 5. Mulank 2 is Anti-Numbers or Non-Compatible Number of Mulank 5.

Akashic Records give Remedies to the Problems of Life, which are created on the account of bad Karma of present Life and the past lives. Simplest Remedy is Forgiveness for mistakes. Meditation reveals, the Secrets of the Life, and of the Universe. Manifestation is the best Remedy. Changing the Mindset and Lifestyle are also very good Remedies.

Remedy(s) is/are to be done, for the Anti-Number(s), by pleasing these Anti-Number(s) associated Planet(s), as mentioned in the Chapter 1, or by pleasing the gods associated with these Planets by regular prayers, chanting and worshipping, or regular offerings to these Planets or the gods, or doing the right rituals everyday or right day(s), in order to placate them (associated Planets, associated gods), and make them happy.

Remedies:

Go for long drive. Go to plants nursery quite often. Put lots of plants in the surrounding. Make Air (Vaayu) and Earth (Prithvi) elements strong.

Air is an element of North-West (NW). Have Doors and Windows, as per the Vaastu for proper ventilation in the House or the Home.

Earth is the first and foremost element of the Nature. Consult the Land for its Energy, Area, Shape, Direction etc., from a Vaastu Expert before purchasing, and then make a House or Home over it. Soil also matters in the Vaastu.

Best Career/Profession:

For Beings having Mulank 5, best Career or Profession are Finance, Banking Sector, Playwriting, Book Writing, Scriptwriting or Screenwriting, Screenplay writing, Creativity and Innovation, Production House, Business, Marketing, CEO, Top Management, and Travel & Tourism.

Lucky Day:

Lucky Day for Beings having Mulank 5 is Wednesday. Plan and do the activities on Wednesday. Wednesdays falling on 5, 14, and 23 dates of the Month are the luckiest dates. Lucky Days are the favourable days, special days, best days, more beneficial, give additional strength, and bring good news to the beings.

Lucky Month(s) of Years and Lucky Years of Life:

For Beings having Mulank 5, 5th Month May is the Lucky Month. Lucky Years of the Life for Beings having Mulank 5 are 5th year, 14th year, 23rd year, 32nd year, 41st year, 50th year, 59th year, 68th year, 77th year, and the 86th year. Any other year of the life, which is divisible by Number 5 will also be beneficial. Lucky Month(s) and Lucky Years are the favourable month(s) and the years, and bring good news (unexpected financial gains, growth, job, promotion, marriage, children etc.) to the beings. In addition to it, all the years, which add up to 1 or total 1 are also favourable years for the Beings having Mulank 5, like 1st year, 10th year, 19th year, 28th year, 37th year, 46th year, 55th year, 64th year, 73rd year, 82nd year, and the 91st year.

Lucky Colours:

Lucky Colours for Beings having Mulank 5 are all shades of Green Colour, and the lighter shades of Brown, and the White Colours. Beings with Mulank 5 should wear, and keep the things (like Clothing, Pillows and Cushions Covers, Curtains, Drapery, Tablecloths, Bed Sheets etc.) with shades of Green, and the lighter shades of Brown, and the White Colours with themselves, and try remaining in the surroundings of these shades of Green, and the lighter shades of Brown, and the White Colours.

Life itself is the biggest school, and Nature, the best teacher, of Life. If you are clear about What, then How will automatically be taken care of, by the Nature. Give others, their own space, and in turn, they will give you, your own space. Never Give up. Keep the self busy in improving with no time left for criticising the others. Fear is the Death. Knowledge cancels the Fear. Creator lies in the Creation. In the Life, many times, Less is More. Many times, Criticism leads to the Admiration. All the homes are Dark, until the Mother awakes. Life does not change, when we try fixing every piece of it, rather, the Life changes, when we start showing up, exactly what we are. We are the Mountains. In the Darkness of Luck, put Floodlight of Hard Work. It always seems Impossible, until it is done. Do not doubt, but trust the Self. Do not put all eggs in the same Basket. Haters are secret Admirers. Often, see yourself in the Mirror. Mirror means My Error (Mirror = My + Error).

Tourmaline is the Stone of Reconciliation. Tourmaline stone fosters Compassion and cool Headedness.

Tourmaline stone radiates an Energy, which attracts Money, Healing and the Friendship. Tourmaline Stone is used for grounding purposes, i.e. for Stabilising (reaffirming our Earth Roots).

End is the Beginning.

Mulank 6

Beings, which are born on 6, 15 or 24 of any month, have Mulank 6. Mulank 6 or the Number 6 is ruled and influenced by the Shukra or the Planet Venus. Number 6 is a Good Number. It is the Number of Love, Motherhood and Fatherhood. Number 6 is the most Loving, Sharing & Caring, and Surviving of all Numbers. Venus refers to, "I want". Planet Venus spins slowly in the opposite direction from most other Planets. Venus is quite similar in structure and size to the Planet Earth. Planet Venus is also called as, "Earth's Evil Twin". Thick atmosphere of Planet Venus traps heat in a runaway Greenhouse Effect, and thus, Planet Venus is the hottest planet in our Solar System. Surface temperature of Planet Venus is hot enough to melt the Lead. Venus represents Values, i.e. Receptiveness, Intake and Harmony. Venus is the Planet of Love, Romance, Money, Beauty, and the Art. Shukra or the Venus is feminine in its very nature. Venus is the Planet of Luck. Beings having Mulank 6 are quite lucky beings. Beings having Mulank 6 are Encouraging and Comforting in their nature. The Order of Effectiveness and Prominence of Number 6 is, "24 < 6 < 15".

Characteristics - Strengths and Weaknesses of Beings born with Mulank 6 are as follows:

Strengths:

Beings with Mulank 6 have very Good, Magnetic and Charismatic Personality, and they get all possible Help, Support and Guidance, whenever they need it. Beings with Mulank 6 are Respectable, Gentle, Soft-spoken, Aesthete, Artist, Artiste, Connoisseur, Sensual, Youthful & Romantic (easily attracted by the opposite Sex), Luxury Seeker, Secretive, and love pleasant things. Beings having Mulank 6 are quite averse to Mismanagement, Chaos & Disorder, and Ugly & Dirty things, Beings having Mulank 6 are caring by their Nature. Beings with Mulank 6 are Family-oriented beings, and take full care of their Children. Beings having Mulank 6 possess refined Tastes, and are Lucky enough to live in full Luxury and Modernity from early age of their Life. In some cases, they are also Heir to large Fortunes. Number 6 is a Good Number as Psychic Number.

Weaknesses:

Strengths of beings are also beings Weaknesses. Beings having Mulank 6 have health-related issues. Beings having Mulank 6 cannot say No. Beings having Mulank are quite Lazy and Indolent; as a result, they do not complete their things on time, and thus, suffer huge losses, including the Financial Losses. These beings are afraid of facing the Challenges of the Life. Also, these beings having Mulank 6 can't bear being by themselves. Thus, these beings constantly seek somebody's company. Beings having Mulank 6 easily get triggered and turn angry, when the things are not properly managed according to them. They are fussy beings.

Friend-Number(s):

Jupiter, Uranus, Mercury, Saturn, and the Mars are the friendly planets of the Venus. Beings, which are ruled by these Planets, viz. Jupiter, Uranus, Mercury, Saturn, and the

Mars, remain in harmony with Mulank 6 beings. Thus, for beings having Mulank 6, beings having Mulanks 3, 4, 5, 8 and 9 are friends. Mulanks 3, 4, 5, 8 and 9 are Friend-Numbers or Compatible Numbers of Mulank 6.

Anti-Number(s) and Remedies:

Sun, Moon and Neptune are unfriendly to the Planet Venus. Therefore, beings with Mulank or Numbers 1, 2, 6 and 7 are not friendly for beings having Mulank 6. Mulanks 1, 2, 6 and 7 are Anti-Numbers or Non-Compatible Numbers of Mulank 6.

Akashic Records give Remedies to the Problems of Life, which are created on the account of bad Karma of present Life and the past lives. Simplest Remedy is Forgiveness for mistakes. Meditation reveals, the Secrets of the Life, and of the Universe. Manifestation is the best Remedy. Changing the Mindset and Lifestyle are also very good Remedies.

Remedy(s) is/are to be done, for the Anti-Number(s), by pleasing these Anti-Number(s) associated Planet(s), as mentioned in the Chapter 1, or by pleasing the gods associated with these Planets by regular prayers, chanting and worshipping, or regular offerings to these Planets or the gods, or doing the right rituals everyday or right day(s), in order to placate them (associated Planets, associated gods), and make them happy.

Remedies:

Make Air, Water, Fire and Earth elements strong.

Make Air element strong. Air is an element of North-West (NW). Have Doors and Windows, as per the Vaastu for proper ventilation in the House or the Home.

Make Water element strong. Have Water Taps, Hand-pump, Well(if), Swimming Pool, or put a Spring or Waterfall or Sea or River Painting or an Aquarium in the North-East (NE) Direction of the House or the Home, as per the Vaastu.

Make Fire element strong. Have Kitchen, or put a Fire Painting or a Flame or Electrical Gadget(s) in the South-East (SE) Direction of the House or the Home, as per the Vaastu.

Make Earth element strong. Earth is the first and foremost element of the Nature. Consult the Land for its Energy, Area, Shape, Direction etc., from a Vaastu Expert before purchasing, and then make a House or Home over it. Soil also matters in the Vaastu.

Best Career/Profession:

For Beings having Mulank 6, best Career or Profession relates to the Politics, Business, Hotel Industry, Media & Mass Communication, Law, Creativity, Fine Arts (Painting, Sculpture, Music, and Dance), Filming & Entertainment, Writing, Interior Designing, Glamour, Beauty & Cosmetics, and Jewellery-Making.

Lucky Day:

Lucky Day for Beings having Mulank 6 is Friday. Plan and do activities on Friday. Fridays falling on 3, 6, 9, 12, 15, 18, 21, 24, 27, and 30 dates of the Month are the luckiest dates. Lucky Days are the favourable days, special days, best days, more beneficial, give additional strength, and bring good news to the beings.

Lucky Month(s) of Years and Lucky Years of Life:

For Beings having Mulank 6, 6th Month June is the Lucky Month. Lucky Years of the Life for Beings having Mulank 6 are 6th year, 15th year, 24th year, 33rd year, 42nd year, 51st year, 60th year, 63rd year, 69th year, and the 78th year. Any other year of the life, which is divisible by Number 6 will also be beneficial. Lucky Month(s) and Lucky Years are the favourable month(s) and the years, and bring good news (unexpected financial gains, growth, job, promotion, marriage, children etc.) to the beings.

Lucky Colours:

Lucky Colours for Beings having Mulank 6 is White. White is the Colour of planet Venus. White is the Colour of Success. Beings with Mulank 6 should wear, and keep the things (like Clothing, Pillows and Cushions Covers, Curtains, Drapery, Tablecloths, Bed Sheets etc.) with White Colours with themselves, and try remaining in the surroundings of White Colour. Other alternative colours but lesser in the order of effectiveness and prominence than the White Colour for the beings having Mulank 6 are Chrome Yellow, Light Blue and the Pink.

Success Stories are written, only after, the Success has been achieved. Without Trust and Love, Life cannot go on. Success can only be defined in terms of Love, Health and the Happiness. The very purpose of Spirituality is to add goodness and the meaning to the Journey of Life. Live the Life like a Red Rose, full blooded, representing the Love, the Beauty, the Courage, the Respect, and the Admiration. Anything, which is physical, will die a day, and the thing, which is non-physical, i.e. spiritual, will stay forever. Do not be a riff-raff.

CHAPTER EIGHT

Mulank 7

Beings, which are born on 7, 16 or 25 of any month, have Mulank 7. Mulank 7 or the Number 7 is ruled and influenced by the Chandrama and/or Ketu, or the Planets Moon and/or Neptune, respectively. Ketu is South Node of the Planet Moon. Ketu is a shadow planet. Number 7 is a Good Number. Number 7 is a Psychic Number. Number 7 is a Mysterious Number. Number 7 is Number of the Spirituality. Moon refers to, "I feel". Neptune refers to, "I dream". Chandrama or Moon represents the Inner Being or the Inner Self, which is the subconscious repository of Thoughts, Memories, Emotions, and other aspects of the Mind, and make us what we are. Inner being is Feelings, Reactions and the Soul-development. Neptune represents the Integration (the universal ocean of oneness with all beings), i.e. Beyond the Individual (Beyond the Blood-my biggest family; a bestseller Book by Dr. Yaduvir Singh), Obligation and the Loss of Distinction. Moon is the Planet of Love. Moon is a Loyal Companion. Ketu or Neptune is the Planet of the Universal Love. Neptune intensifies Intuition. Neptune teaches all of us to be deeply Compassionate. Neptune asks one to sacrifice for the greater good or for love of the other. Neptune refines, purifies, and also, cleanses; thus, mere vicinity of Planet

Neptune makes a thing pure and purer. Neptune is Idealistic, highly Compassionate and Imaginative. Moon is Feminine in its Nature, i.e. Classy, Traditional, Sensitive & Emotional, and Family-oriented. Ketu has Body, but no Head. Ketu is Artistic in its Nature, but also Incredulous and Sceptical; therefore Ketu is directionless. Ketu creates Doubts. Due to the influence of the Planet Moon, beings having Mulank 7, are the Healers, and provide useful Guidance to the others. Due to the influence of the Planet Neptune, beings having Mulank 7 are Givers, Thinkers and the Philosophers.

Characteristics - Strengths and Weaknesses of Beings born with Mulank 7 are as follows:

Strengths:

Beings with Mulank 7 are Perfectionists and Winners. Beings with Mulank 7 are Healers. Beings having Mulank 7 are quite Creative, and are very good Speakers. Beings having Mulank 7 are quite Convincing and Mobilising, therefore, they easily win the arguments and the situations. Beings having Mulank 7 easily win victories over their enemies. Beings having Mulank 7 are Unconventional. Beings having Mulank 7 are mentally very strong, with good power of Intuition. Beings having Mulank 7 have lots of interest in Yoga and Meditation. Beings with Mulank 7 remain anxious to know more and more about the future. Beings with Mulank 7 are not Wealth and Money Greedy.

Weaknesses:

Strengths of beings are also beings Weaknesses. There may be some difficulties in the life of the beings, born with Mulank 7. Beings having Mulank 7 are Lazy beings. Beings having Mulank 7 are Moody and quite Uncertain, and often these beings have Mood Swings. At times, beings with Mulank 7 do the works without Thinking. Beings having Mulank 7 think more, and are Obsessive in their Nature with excessively busy Minds and hyperactive Brains; therefore, these beings develop Anxiety. Beings having Mulank 7 are Restless beings. Beings having Mulank 7 may be considered as Unfortunate, as these beings meet many Failures in their Lives.

Friend-Number(s):

Sun, Moon, Uranus, and the Mercury are the friendly Planets of Neptune. Beings, which are ruled by these Planets, viz. Sun, Moon, Uranus, and the Mercury, remain in harmony with Mulank 7 beings. Thus, for beings having Mulank 7, beings having Mulanks 1, 2, 4 and 5 are Friends. Mulanks 1, 2, 4 and 5 are Friend-Numbers or Compatible Numbers of Mulank 7.

Anti-Number(s) and Remedies:

Jupiter, Venus, Saturn and Mars are Unfriendly to Neptune. Therefore, beings with Mulank or Numbers 3, 6, 7, 8 and 9 are not friendly for beings having Mulank 7. Mulanks 3, 6, 7, 8 and 9 are Anti-Numbers or Non-Compatible Numbers of Mulank 7.

Akashic Records give Remedies to the Problems of Life, which are created on the account of bad Karma of present Life and the past lives. Simplest Remedy is Forgiveness for mistakes. Meditation reveals, the Secrets of the Life, and of the Universe. Manifestation is the best Remedy. Changing the Mindset and Lifestyle are also very good Remedies.

Remedy(s) is/are to be done, for the Anti-Number(s), by pleasing these Anti-Number(s) associated Planet(s), as mentioned in the Chapter 1, or by pleasing the gods associated with these Planets by regular prayers, chanting and worshipping, or regular offerings to these Planets or the gods, or doing the right rituals everyday or right day(s), in order to placate them (associated Planets, associated gods), and make them happy.

Remedies:

Make Fire element strong. Have Kitchen, or put a Fire Painting or a Flame or Electrical Gadget(s) in the South-East (SE) Direction of the House or the Home, as per the Vaastu.

Best Career/Profession:

For Beings having Mulank 7, best Career or Profession are Planning, Strategy Making, Share Marketing, Gambling, Service & Trading Businesses including Import & Export. Petrochemicals, Dentistry, Research & Development, and Scientist.

Lucky Day:

Lucky Day for Beings having Mulank 7 is Monday. Plan and do activities on Monday. Mondays falling on 7, 16 and 25 dates of the Month are the luckiest dates. Lucky Days are the favourable days, special days, best days, more beneficial, give additional strength, and bring good news to the beings.

Lucky Month(s) of Years and Lucky Years of Life:

For Beings having Mulank 7, 7th Month July is the Lucky Months. Lucky Years of the Life for Beings having Mulank 7 are 7th year, 16th year, 25th year, 34th year, 43rd year, 52nd year, 61st year, 70th year, and the 79th year. Also, 10th year, 19th year, 28th year, 37th year, 46th year, 55th year, 64th year, 73rd year and 82nd Years of Life are favourable years for the Beings having Mulank 7. Also, any other year of the Life, which is divisible by Number 7 will also be Beneficial. Lucky Months and Lucky Years are the favourable months and the years, and bring good news (unexpected financial gains, growth, job, promotion, marriage, children etc.) to the beings.

Lucky Colours:

Lucky Colours for Beings having Mulank 7 are Grey Green and Smoky Brown. Beings with Mulank 7 should wear, and keep the things (like Clothing, Pillows and Cushions Covers, Curtains, Drapery, Tablecloths, Bed Sheets etc.) with Grey Green and Smoky Brown Colours with themselves, and try remaining in the surroundings of these Grey Green and Smoky Brown Colours. Beings having Mulank 7 should avoid things of Black Colours.

Never lose Hope in the Life. We all have got to where the God is, by dint of sheer good karma. The purpose of life can be understood by moonlighting the Spirituality. "Life of Purpose", is the very purpose of the Life. Beings successes or failures are writ large because of the lack of spirituality in their lives. Never tom-tom your physical success and the achievements, as these are temporary and unreal. Have a qualia of "Being Good and Displaying the Goodness". Do not be up in arms. Desire is the root cause of all Sorrows. Keep no Expectations from the others. Avoid Off-putting and Smirking. Always be ready to tide over the others. What is not right and good, pooh-pooh it. Feel Empty, with the Feeling of Fulfillment. Service (Sewa), Love (Prem) and Dedication (Samarpan) are the three fundamental elements of a good Life. DNA holds the Information in the form of Vibrations. Be Infusive. Do not fritter away the Life. Put pants on one leg at a time.

CHAPTER NINE

Mulank 8

Beings, which are born on 8, 17 or 26 of any month, have Mulank 8. Mulank 8 or the Number 8 is ruled and influenced by the Shani, or the Planet Saturn. Number 8 has its shape as two stacked Circles, which represents Heaven and the Earth. Number 8 represents the balance between the Spiritual World and the Material World. Number 8 is number of Banking and Commerce. Number 8 is not a good Number. Number 8 is not a good Psychic Number. Saturn refers to, "I take seriously". Saturn represents the Structure, i.e. Form, Protection Responsibility and the Limitation. Saturn is Dark and Wise. Saturn is Comfortable with the routine Works, and allows no Nonsense. Beings having Mulank 8 are quite Fair-minded, i.e. Fair and Reasonable, and Listen to other being's Opinions. Beings having Mulank 8, wish to bring Changes in the World.

Characteristics - Strengths and Weaknesses of Beings born with Mulank 8 are as follows:

Strengths:

Beings having Mulank 8 are Generous, Brave & Powerful, Determined & Confident. Beings having Mulank 8 can very easily face the Challenges of Life. Beings with Mulank 8 pay heed to the advice of their mentor or the Guru, and execute the same in their lives. Beings having

Mulank 8 have very strong Willpower. Beings having Mulank 4 are Judgemental. Beings having Mulank 6 are Ambitious, and Money-conscious, but not Money-minded. These beings do big things in their Life. For beings having Mulank 8, "Work is the Worship".

Weaknesses:

Strengths of beings are also beings Weaknesses. Beings having Mulank 8 face many difficulties in their lives. Beings having Mulank 8 have Chequered, Unexpected and Unpredictable Life, with many ups and downs, and varied fortunes, which keeps them busy adjusting to the new situations and the circumstances. These beings are unable to reach the top of their job or the career. Beings having Mulank 8 have serious nature.

Friend-Number(s):

Moon, Jupiter, Mercury, Venus and Mars are the friendly Planets of Saturn. Beings, which are ruled by these Planets, viz. Moon, Jupiter, Mercury, Venus and Mars remain in harmony with Mulank 8 beings. Thus, for beings having Mulank 8, beings having Mulanks 2, 3, 5, 6 and 9 are Friends. Mulanks 2, 3, 5, 6 and 9 are Friend - Numbers or Compatible Numbers of Mulank 8.

Anti-Number(s) and Remedies:

Sun, Uranus and Neptune are unfriendly to the Planet Saturn. Therefore, beings with Mulank or Numbers 1, 4, 7, and 8 are not friendly for beings having Mulank 8. Mulanks 1, 4, 7, and 8 are Anti-Numbers or Non-Compatible Numbers of Mulank 8.

Akashic Records give Remedies to the Problems of Life, which are created on the account of bad Karma of present Life and the past lives. Simplest Remedy is Forgiveness for mistakes. Meditation reveals, the Secrets of the Life, and of the Universe. Manifestation is the best Remedy. Changing the Mindset and Lifestyle are also very good Remedies.

Remedy(s) is/are to be done, for the Anti-Number(s), by pleasing these Anti-Number(s) associated Planet(s), as mentioned in the Chapter 1, or by pleasing the gods associated with these Planets by regular prayers, chanting and worshipping, or regular offerings to these Planets or the gods, or doing the right rituals everyday or right day(s), in order to placate them (associated Planets, associated gods), and make them happy.

Remedies:

Make Air element strong. Air is an element of North-West (NW). Have Doors and Windows, as per the Vaastu for proper ventilation in the House or the Home.

Best Career/Profession:

For Beings having Mulank 8, best Career or Profession are Dentist, Scientist, Judiciary, Gambler, Strategic Planning and Management, Trading, Share Market, Import and Export Businesses, Petrochemicals. Beings having Mulank 8 do private jobs.

Lucky Day:

Lucky Day for Beings having Mulank 8 is Saturday. Plan and do activities on Saturday. Saturdays falling on 8 or 17 or 26 dates of the Month are the luckiest dates. Lucky Days are the favourable days, special days, best days, more beneficial, give additional strength, and bring good news to the beings.

Lucky Month(s) of Years and Lucky Years of Life:

For Beings having Mulank 8, 8th Month August is the Lucky Month. Lucky Years of the Life for Beings having Mulank 8 are 8th year, 17th year, 26th year, 35th year, 44th year, 53rd year, 62nd year, 71st year, 80th year and the 89th year. These years are beneficial to beings having Mulank 8, in terms of unexpected gains, jobs, promotions, children and family, marriages etc.. Any other year of the life, which is divisible by Number 8 will also be quite beneficial. Lucky Months and Lucky Years are the favourable months and the years, and bring good news (unexpected financial gains, growth, job, promotion, marriage, children etc.) to the beings.

Lucky Colours:

Lucky Colour for Beings having Mulank 8 are Grey, Purple, Dark Blue and Black. Beings with Mulank 8 should wear, and keep the things (like Clothing, Pillows and Cushions Covers, Curtains, Drapery, Tablecloths, Bed Sheets etc.) with Grey, Purple, Dark Blue and Black Colours with themselves, and try remaining in the surroundings of Grey, Purple, Dark Blue and Black Colours only.

Life is a Stage, already set by the Nature, the God, for each one us, and, no changes can be made therein by anybody. Sit in front of this Stage of Life. Lights will flicker, as the people, situations, events and circumstances will sway and dance on the Stage of Life. The bass will thump deep into the chest. Vibrations will resonate through the bones. But, we as the beings, should crave for more, more and more, as the Music of the Life on this Stage of Life was not just the vibrations, but a rhythm, beats & emotions, woven into the notes of this Music of the Life. And soon, the heart will leap with the Joy. It is called, "embracing the Life".

All limitations reside within the Mind. Choose the freedom. Freedom is the Life. Life is all good, and limitless.

Mix efforts and courage with purpose and direction. What is being said, is Advertising, and what remain unsaid, is News. When it seems that something is wrong in the Life, it's better to get its spirituality check-up, as a stitch in time saves nine. Hedonia (immediate sensory pleasure, happiness, and enjoyment) and Eudaimonia (consequences of self-growth and self-actualization) both, are very important in Life. There are many happenstances in the Life. Have motto "Carpe diem," and carefully contrive to live down to it, without riding roughshod over. God has arranged flat bread for all. With halcyon days of the Life, we all are on an idyllic sojourn on the planet Earth.

CHAPTER TEN

Mulank 9

Beings, which are born on 9, 18 or 27 of any month, have Mulank 9. Mulank 9 or the Number 9 is ruled and influenced by the Mangal or the Planet Mars. Mars was named by the Romans for their God of War due its Red Colour, which is reminiscent of Blood. Mars is also called as the "Red Planet". Mars has Red Colour due to Iron deposits and Iron Rust. Number 9 is a good number. Number 9 holds a very significant and a powerful position in the Numerology. Number 9 is a fortunate number. Number 9 is the Number of Power. Number 9 is a humanitarian number. Number 9 brings lots of good luck. Number 9 denotes the completeness, i.e. finality of the existing phase, and the beginning of a new phase in the life. Number 9 is the end number of the Series, i.e. the Series on which, all our materialistic calculations are done/based. Mars refers to, "I act". Mars represents Action, i.e. Self-projection, Ambition and Impulse. Mars refers to the Strength, Masculinity and the Leadership. Beings having Mulank 9 are Go-getters and they believe in direct approach in all their works, and tolerate no nonsense. Beings having Mulank 9 are quite enterprising. Beings having Mulank 9 are determined to succeed. Beings having Mulank 9 never give up. The Order of Effectiveness and Prominence of Number 9 is, "27 < 18 <

9".

Characteristics - Strengths and Weaknesses of Beings born with Mulank 9 are as follows:

Strengths:

Beings with Mulank 9 are Idealists, Energetic, Ambitious, Emotional, Courageous, Outspoken, Aggressive, Stubborn and possess very strong Willpower. They are like a coconut-hard on the outside, but sweet and pulpy from inside. Beings having Mulank 9 have good personality with a very strong determination, and they do good and rapid progress on their chosen path(s) of the Life. Beings with Mulank 9 remain grounded to the Earth. Beings having Mulank 9, earn good name and fame in their Life. They are quite inspirational. Outwardly, beings having Mulank 9 are very hard and harshly Disciplined, and also, seemingly Unshakeable, but inwardly they are very Soft and Compassionate.

Weaknesses:

Strengths of beings are also beings Weaknesses. Beings having Mulank 9 are quite Short-tempered and carry anger on their nose. Beings having Mulank 9 don't keep things in their hearts. Beings having Mualnk 9 have tendency to indulge with the opposite sex, but they should avoid it, as it is harmful, and brings bad name, and also, huge loss to them.

Friend-Number(s):

Sun, Moon, Jupiter, Uranus, Mercury and Venus are the friendly Planets of the Mars. Beings, which are ruled by these Planets, viz. Sun, Moon, Jupiter, Uranus, Mercury and Venus, remain in harmony with Mulank 9 beings. Thus, for beings having Mulank 9, beings having Mulanks 1, 2, 3, 4, 5 and 6 are Friends. Mulanks 1, 2, 3, 4, 5, 6 and 9 are Friend-Numbers or Compatible Numbers of Mulank 9.

Anti-Number(s) and Remedies:

Neptune and Saturn are unfriendly to the Mars. Therefore, beings with Mulank or Numbers 7 and 8 are not friendly for beings having Mulank 9. Mulanks 7 and 8 are Anti-Numbers or Non-Compatible Numbers of Mulank 9.

Akashic Records give Remedies to the Problems of Life, which are created on the account of bad Karma of present Life and the past lives. Simplest Remedy is Forgiveness for mistakes. Meditation reveals, the Secrets of the Life, and of the Universe. Manifestation is the best Remedy. Changing the Mindset and Lifestyle are also very good Remedies.

Remedy(s) is/are to be done, for the Anti-Number(s), by pleasing these Anti-Number(s) associated Planet(s), as mentioned in the Chapter 1, or by pleasing the gods associated with these Planets by regular prayers, chanting and worshipping, or regular offerings to these Planets or the gods, or doing the right rituals everyday or right day(s), in order to placate them (associated Planets, associated gods), and make them happy.

Remedies:

Make Fire element strong. Have Kitchen, or put a Fire Painting or a Flame or Electrical Gadget(s) in the South-East (SE) Direction of the House or the Home, as per the Vaastu.

Best Career/Profession:

For Beings having Mulank 9, best Career or Profession are Civil Services, Police Force, Defense Services (Air Force, Army and Navy), Surgeon and the Sports.

Lucky Day:

Lucky Day for Beings having Mulank 9 is Tuesday. Plan and do activities on Tuesday. Tuesdays falling on 3 or 6 or 9 or 12 or 15 or 18 or 21 or 24 or 27 or 30 dates of the Month are the luckiest dates. Lucky Days are the favourable days, special days, best days, more beneficial, give additional strength, and bring good news to the beings.

Lucky Month(s) of Years and Lucky Years of Life:

For Beings having Mulank 9, 9th Month September is the Lucky Month. Lucky Years of the Life for Beings having Mulank 9 are 9th year, 18th year, 27th year, 36th year, 45th year, 54th year, 63rd year, 72nd year, 81st year, 90th and the 99th year. More specifically, years 27th, 36th and the 45th are quite significant. These years are beneficial to beings having Mulank 9, in terms of unexpected gains, jobs, promotions, children and family, marriages etc.. Any other year of the life, which is divisible by Number 9 will also be beneficial. Lucky Months and Lucky Years are the favourable months and the years, and bring good news (unexpected financial gains, growth, job, promotion, marriage, children etc.) to the beings.

Lucky Colours:

Lucky Colour for Beings having Mulank 9 are Red, and all shades of Red and Pink. Planet Mars is of Red Colour. Beings with Mulank 9 should wear, and keep the things (like Clothing, Pillows and Cushions Covers, Curtains, Drapery, Tablecloths, Bed Sheets etc.) with Red and Pink Colours with themselves, and try remaining in the surroundings of these Red or Pink Colours, or their shades.

Life sometimes unexpectedly forces us to terminate one project and focus on a new one. Tort Law is executed by the Nature in the Life. Get au fait with the laws of Nature. Nothing is fait accompli in the Life. Life is a necessary myth. Bad Karma, which is being earned, is a man-made disaster, and society-sponsored murder of one's Life's quality; which simply ruins the Life and upsets the Life processes. In the Life, there should be no data cherry-picking and cherry-picking analyses, as it simply leads to the formation of the biases, resulting in elimination of neutrality and purity in the Life. Life process is no run-of-the-mill; as it only makes this whole existence to exist. Though it is never late for a being for going into action for Spirituality, however early is always better for the Life, Nature and the whole creation. Keep moonlighting for the Spirituality in the Journey of Life. Most of us, have mistakenly repurposed the Life for all that, which is too trivial, ephemeral, non-existent and too insignificant. Spirituality turns the tide, of the bad in the Life. Practice the Spirituality, and then, enjoy how this is all panning out. Never wax lyrical about your physical and spiritual attainments/accomplishments in the Life. Never turn a blind eye to what is real & genuine, and just & equitable. Always be ready to subserve the every other entity in this Nature and the existence, i.e. the God's creation. Make your this Journey of the Life, pièce de résistance. We are, what we eat. God is an expression of the collective consciousness. Display largesse to everyone; full monty. An act of kindness makes the peace and happiness writ large. Prayer is the best antidote.

Bhagyank 1

Bhagyank 1 is the Number of Practicality, Leadership, Overall Success and Achievements.

Characteristics - Strengths and Weaknesses of Beings born with Bhagyank 1 are as follows:

Strengths:

Beings with Bhagyank 1 are associated with the qualities of Sun, like Optimism, Self-reliance, and a strong inclination to help the others. Beings having Bhagyank 1 are Clever, Focussed, Creative, Logical and Continuous Learners. They keep smiling. Beings with Bhagyank 1 are go-getters, and take initiative(s).

Weaknesses:

Strengths of beings are also beings weaknesses. Beings with Bhagyank 1 are Egotist. At times, they are super confused. Beings having Bhagyank 1 are natural leaders, but should balance their confidence with humility to avoid arrogance.

Friend-Number(s):

Beings having Bhagyank 1 are compatible and friendly with other beings having Bhagyank 1, 2, 3, 4, 5, 7 and 9. Bhagyank 1 beings have similar vibrations; therefore they are suitable for marriage, or friendship and business partnership. Bhagyank 1 beings will always have good relationships with beings having Bhagyank 2, therefore they can marry each other. Bhagyank 1 and 3 beings can marry each other, and do some business in partnership. Bhagyank 1 and 4 beings can marry each other, and do some business in partnership. Bhagyank 1 beings will always have good relationships with beings having Bhagyank 5, therefore they can marry each other. Bhagyank 1 and 7 beings can marry each other and can do some business in partnership. Bhagyank 1 and 9 beings, both have positive vibrations and energy; therefore they have harmonious relationship(s). Bhagyank 1 and 9 beings are made for each other, and can enter into any kind of sweet and eternal relationship, whether marriage, or business partnership, or anything else.

Anti-Number(s) and Remedies:

Beings having Bhagyank 1 are non-compatible and unfriendly with other beings having Bhagyank 6 and 8. Bhagyank 1 beings will always have bad relationship(s) with beings having Bhagyank 6. Bhagyank 6 and 8 beings can never have good bonding. Bhagyank 1 beings should never marry or do a business in partnership with beings having Bhagyank 6 and 8.

Akashic Records give Remedies to the Problems of Life, which are created on the account of bad Karma of present Life and the past lives. Simplest Remedy is Forgiveness for mistakes. Meditation reveals, the Secrets of the Life, and of the Universe. Manifestation is the best Remedy. Changing the Mindset and Lifestyle are also very good Remedies.

Remedy(s) is/are to be done, for the Anti-Number(s), by pleasing these Anti-Number(s) associated Planet(s), as mentioned in the Chapter 1, or by pleasing the gods associated with these Planets by regular prayers, chanting and worshipping, or regular offerings to these Planets or the gods, or doing the right rituals everyday or right day(s), in order to placate them (associated Planets, associated gods), and make them happy.

Remedies-Beings having Bhagyank 1 must align themselves with the Sun, in order to better the health and becoming prosperous. Work in natural sunlight. Eat meals on time. Maintain clean environment.

Best Career/Profession:

For Beings having Bhagyank 1, best Career or Profession are Business, Politics, Civil Services, Diplomat, Head of Organisation, Director, Manager and Public Relations. Any Career/Profession is good for the beings having Bhagyank 1, provided they have good control on their ego.

The Nature and the Creation, create us, to in turn create themselves. In the Life, at times, one closes only counts in horseshoes and hand grenades; it is the destiny. Nature serves summons of quo warranto on us from time to time for wrongdoings. It is really good, when someone prays for us, without we come to know about it. It is the highest form of respect and care. Never ship down. Existence does poetic justice with all without any exception and discrimination. Life is grand touring on rodshaving undulations. Do not get cold feet in trying something new and exciting. Expect the unexpected in the game of the Life. Get "the Best" from every present moment, without thinking for tomorrow, as today only makes the tomorrow. Tomorrow cannot be Good, if Today is not the Best. Have no truck with that, which is simply not good. Life is a boisterous, rambunctious merrymaking, carefree antics, and the horseplay, without any schmaltz. Journey of the Life is curate's egg; a mixed bag. Dig your heels in on certain points, that you think, are, Just, Ethical and Right. Stay fired up; otherwise Life is a ho-hum script. Thoughts and the Actions will stand us in good stead, when it comes to creating Karma. Facultative adjustment in the Life is quite essential in relation to the one's abilities. We all are skating on thin ice. Keep looking up; it is the secret of Life. Always, believe and remember that the potential within us is much greater than the obstacles around us.

CHAPTER TWELVE

Bhagyank 2

Bhagyank 2 is the Number of Flexibility.

Characteristics - Strengths and Weaknesses of Beings born with Bhagyank 2 are as follows:

Strengths:

Beings having Bhagyank 2 are Faithful, Amiable, Amicable, Friendly, Suave, Naive, Gentle, Kind-hearted, Caring, Cooperative and quite Helpful. They are Melomaniac or Musicophile, i.e. Music Lovers. Beings having Bhagyank 2 maintain relations in the Life.

Weaknesses:

Strengths of beings are also beings weaknesses. Beings with Bhagyank 2 create problems for themselves by over-attaching with the others. Beings with Bhagyank 2 very easily catch negativity, and also, get badly influenced by it.

Friend-Number(s):

Beings having Bhagyank 2 are compatible and friendly with other beings having Bhagyank 1, 3, 4, 7, 8 and 9. Bhagyank 2 beings will always have good relationships with beings having Bhagyank 1, therefore they can marry each other, or become good friends or start and run a business in partnership. Bhagyank 2 and 3 beings can marry each other and do some business in partnership. This combination is good. Bhagyank 2 and 4 beings can marry each other and do some business in partnership. Bhagyank 2 beings will always have good relationships with beings having Bhagyank 7, therefore they can marry each other. Bhagyank 2 and 7 beings exude cordiality in their relationships and produce much positive results. Bhagyank 2 and 8 beings, attract each other. Both have positive vibrations and energy, therefore can go for any kind of relationship. Bhagyank 2 and 9 beings have positive vibrations and energy. Bhagyank 2 and 9 beings can enter into any kind of sweet and eternal relationship, whether marriage, or business partnership, or friendship, anything else.

Anti-Number(s) and Remedies:

Beings having Bhagyank 2 are non-compatible and unfriendly with other beings having Bhagyank 2, 5 and 6. Bhagyank 2 beings will always have bad relationships with beings having Bhagyank 2. Bhagyank 2 and 5 beings can never have good bonding; therefore, they must desist from, marrying each other, or doing a business in partnership, or even friendship. Bhagyank 2 and 6 beings can never have good bonding, and therefore, should avoid entering into any kind of relationship.

Akashic Records give Remedies to the Problems of Life, which are created on the account of bad Karma of present Life and the past lives. Simplest Remedy is Forgiveness for mistakes. Meditation reveals, the Secrets of the Life, and of the Universe. Manifestation is the best Remedy. Changing the Mindset and Lifestyle are also very good Remedies.

Remedy(s) is/are to be done, for the Anti-Number(s), by pleasing these Anti-Number(s) associated Planet(s), as mentioned in the Chapter 1, or by pleasing the gods associated with these Planets by regular prayers, chanting and worshipping, or regular offerings to these Planets or the gods, or doing the right rituals everyday or right day(s), in order to placate them (associated Planets, associated gods), and make them happy.

Remedies-Beings having Bhagyank 2 must align themselves with the Moon. These Beings should resist emotional fluctuations, and maintain Stability in their Life. These Beings must socialise themselves. Also, these Beings having Bhagyank 2 should work on their personal growth and visibility.

Best Career/Profession:

For Beings having Bhagyank 2, best Career or Profession are Engineering, Communication, Advertisement Agency, Diplomacy, Media, Marketing, Travel and Tourism, Hotel Industry, Hospitality, Care Industry, Theatre, Movies, Fine Arts and International Trading.

Parapraxis or the Freudian Slip, in Psychoanalysis, is an "Error" in the Speech, or the Memory, or a Physical Action, which occurs due to interference of an unconscious subdued wish or a desire, or due to the internal train of thoughts. Parapraxis or the Freudian Slip is a "Slip" of the tongue, or the pen, or forgetfulness, or misplacement of objects, or other error(s), which reveal the unconscious wishes, attitudes and impulses. Life is a curate's egg. Value the self-peace, over other's opinion. Develop the ability to make the Infinity out of the Zero. Every being has talent; just courage is needed to follow it, through the seemingly darker paths of the Life. Consistency is the key to Success. Normal beings are ignorant and totally unaware of the Arcana of the Life. Life should be hunky-dory. Other than the Life itself, there is no other overarching issue in the Life. Do not gaslight the others.

Bhagyank 3

Bhagyank 3 is the Number of Creativity.

Characteristics - Strengths and Weaknesses of Beings born with Bhagyank 3 are as follows:

Strengths:

Beings having Bhagyank 3 have very Bright Mind, and a very strong Willpower. Beings having Bhagyank 3 are quite Positive, and get Success in their life with Dedication, Discipline and Hard Work. They have ability to face any challenge and hard situation of the Life. Beings with Bhagyank can extricate themselves from adverse situations of the Life. They very well gel with the others, and thus, can very efficiently work in a team. Beings having Bhagyank 3 are very sensitive towards others. They have very good friends and enjoy good family life.

Weaknesses:

Strengths of beings are also beings weaknesses. Beings with Bhagyank 3 may create problems for themselves by being over-sensitive to others. They get easily excited about new ideas in haste, overindulge, and can be indecisive. They have scattered energy. They have difficulty in following the routine. Beings having Bhagyank 3 are quite sensitive to criticism.

Friend-Number(s):

Beings having Bhagyank 3 are compatible and friendly with other beings having Bhagyank 1, 2, 3, 5, 6, 8 and 9. Bhagyank 3 beings will always have good relationships with beings having Bhagyank 1; therefore they can marry each other, or become good friends or start and run a business in partnership. Bhagyank 3 beings inspire the beings having Bhagyank 1. Bhagyank 3 and 2 beings can marry each other and do some business in partnership. This combination is good and mutually beneficial. Bhagyank 3 and 3 beings can marry each other and do some business in partnership. This combination goes together and works very well. Bhagyank 3 and 5 beings are compatible to one another. Bhagyank 3 and 5 beings can become very good friends or even marry each other, and / or do some business in partnership. Bhagyank 3 beings will always have good and beneficial relationships with beings having Bhagyank 6. Therefore thay can marry each other as they are quite compatible. They gel very well with each other. Bhagyank 3 and 8 beings exude cordiality in their relationships and produce much positive results. Bhagyank 3 and 8 beings attract each other and can create a very good relationship. Both have positive vibrations and energy, therefore can go for any kind of relationship. They have good bonding and understanding. Bhagyank 3 and 9 beings have positive vibrations and share good energy. Both are good for one another. Bhagyank 3 and 9 beings can enter into any kind of sweet and eternal relationship, whether marriage, or business partnership, or friendship, anything else. They can build a good understanding and bonding.

Anti-Number(s) and Remedies:

Beings having Bhagyank 3 are non-compatible and unfriendly with other beings having Bhagyank 4 and 7. Bhagyank 3 beings will always have bad relationships with beings having Bhagyank 4, and can never become good friends. Therefore, any kind of relationship between the Beings having Bhagyank 3 and 4 should be avoided. Bhagyank 3 and 7 beings can never have good bonding, as their thinking are very different, therefore, they must desist from, marrying each other, or doing a business in partnership, or even friendship.

Akashic Records give Remedies to the Problems of Life, which are created on the account of bad Karma of present Life and the past lives. Simplest Remedy is Forgiveness for mistakes. Meditation reveals, the Secrets of the Life, and of the Universe. Manifestation is the best Remedy. Changing the Mindset and Lifestyle are also very good Remedies.

Remedy(s) is/are to be done, for the Anti-Number(s), by pleasing these Anti-Number(s) associated Planet(s), as mentioned in the Chapter 1, or by pleasing the gods associated with these Planets by regular prayers, chanting and worshipping, or regular offerings to these Planets or the gods, or doing the right rituals everyday or right day(s), in order to placate them (associated Planets, associated gods), and make them happy.

Remedies-Beings having Bhagyank 3 must align themselves with the Jupiter (Guru). These Beings should use Citrine Crystals for attracting opportunities in their Life. Citrine is a beautiful and vibrant crystal. Citrine Crystal is used for establishing a deep connection with the Sun, thus embodying warmth, abundance, and the vitality. Feng Shui (a Chinese System of Laws, which is considered to govern spatial arrangement and the orientation, in relation to the Flow of Energy (Chi)) is recommended for such beings. These Beings must focus on the cleanliness and their digestive health. For mental well-being, better emotional health, overcoming anxiety, stress reduction, minimising distrust on the others and improving the relationships, and also, for improvement of communication skills, such Beings having Bhagyank 3 should do Meditation, Yoga and other physical exercises regularly.

Best Career/Profession:

For Beings having Bhagyank 3, best Career or Profession are Head of Organisation, Research & Development (R&D), Business, Cinema, Actors, Models, Artists, Poets, Travel & Tourism, Publishing Industry and the Music Industry.

One Life is not enough. Life and Time are the best Teachers; Life teaches Use of Time and the Time teaches Value for Life. Time decides who you meet in your Life. Heart decides who you want in your Life. Behaviour decides who will stay in your Life. In Life, some things are better, if left, Unsaid, and Undone. Good Thoughts and Good Deed are the only Talismans, and also, the sine qua non, of a Good and a Well-lived Life. Do not adjourn the Life's good things sine die. Everyone must have their mojo working over throughout their life's journey. The name should have mojo; use Numerology; this Book by Dr. Yaduvir Singh.

CHAPTER FOURTEEN

Bhagyank 4

Bhagyank 4 is the Number of Nature, Health, Career, Love Life and the Friends. Bhagyank 4 is considered lucky for Zodiac signs Leo and Scorpio. Bhagyank 4 is dominated by the planet Uranus.

Characteristics - Strengths and Weaknesses of Beings born with Bhagyank 4 are as follows:

Strengths:

Beings having Bhagyank 4 are very Passionate for their works; therefore they are very Successful in their Career. These beings very easily get all the Luxuries and Comforts of the Life. These beings have very good Mental Strength. They are patient Listeners and Balanced beings. These beings carry a pragmatic view towards the Life, and are not very Materialistic; therefore they lead a Peaceful and Happy, Well-ordered and Well-structured Stable Idyllic Life with extremely Good Relationships. Beings having Bhagyank 4 follow the Rules. Beings having Bhagyank 4 possess exceptional Organisational & Planning Skills and Reasoning & Problem-solving Skills. Beings having Bhagyank 4 are very Stable in almost every Area of their Life.

Weaknesses:

Strengths of beings are also beings weaknesses. Beings with Bhagyank 4 do not make friends easily. Beings with Bhagyank 4 can be over-critical, which may lead to the self-doubt, and thus, attracting negative attention.

Friend-Number(s):

Beings having Bhagyank 4 are compatible and friendly with other beings having Bhagyank 1, 2, 5, 6, 7 and 9. Bhagyank 4 beings will always have good relationships with beings having Bhagyank 1, therefore they can be very good friends or they can marry each other, or can start and run a business in partnership. Bhagyank 4 and 2 beings can marry each other and have a good family, and do some business in partnership. These numbers are harmonious for one another. This combination is good and mutually beneficial. Bhagyank 4 and 2 beings can be very good friends. Bhagyank 3 and 3 beings can marry each other and do some business in partnership. This combination goes together and works very well. Bhagyank 4 and 5 beings are compatible to one another. Bhagyank 4 and 5 beings can enter into a marriage, friendship or business relationships. Bhagyank 4 and 6 beings can become very good friends or even marry each other, and/or do some business in partnership. Bhagyank 4 beings will always have strong bonding and good and beneficial relationships with beings having Bhagyank 6. Therefore they can marry each other as they are quite compatible. Bhagyank 4 and 7 beings complement each other. Bhagyank 4 and 7 beings will have harmony in their relationships. They can marry each other. In business as well, Bhagyank 4 and 7 beings do well together. Bhagyank 4 and 9 beings have positive vibrations and share good energy. Both are good for one another. Bhagyank 4 and 9 beings can enter into any kind of sweet and eternal relationship, whether marriage, or business partnership, or friendship, anything else. They can build a good understanding and bonding.

Anti-Number(s) and Remedies:

Beings having Bhagyank 4 are non-compatible and unfriendly with other beings having Bhagyank 3, 4 and 8. Bhagyank 4 beings will always have bad relationships with beings having Bhagyank 3, and can never become good friends. Therefore, any kind of relationship between the Beings having Bhagyank 4 and 3 should be avoided. Bhagyank 4 and 4 beings can't make a good bonding. Therefore, any kind of relationship between the Beings having Bhagyank 4 and 4 should be avoided. Bhagyank 4 and 8 beings can never have good bonding, as their thinkings are very different, therefore, they must desist from, marrying each other, or doing a business in partnership, or even friendship. Combination of Bhagyank 4 and 8 is not good.

Akashic Records give Remedies to the Problems of Life, which are created on the account of bad Karma of present Life and the past lives. Simplest Remedy is Forgiveness for mistakes. Meditation reveals, the Secrets of the Life, and of the Universe. Manifestation is the best Remedy. Changing the Mindset and Lifestyle are also very good Remedies.

Remedy(s) is/are to be done, for the Anti-Number(s), by pleasing these Anti-Number(s) associated Planet(s), as mentioned in the Chapter 1, or by pleasing the gods associated with these Planets by regular prayers, chanting and worshipping, or regular offerings to these Planets or the gods, or doing the right rituals everyday or right day(s), in order to placate them (associated Planets, associated gods), and make them happy.

Remedies-Beings having Bhagyank 4 must align themselves with the Uranus (Rahu). These Beings should feed the dogs. These Beings must use their intellect and plan out the things effectively. Beings having Bhagyank 4 need to be patient and consistent.

Best Career/Profession:

For Beings having Bhagyank 4, best Career or Profession are Advisors, Counsellors, Agriculture Industry, Coal & Mining, Science & Technology, Engineering, Architecture, and the Builder.

Do not compare your Life, with the Life of the others. They rise and shine at their time, and you, rise and shine at your time. Anger kills the Wisdom, Doubt kills the Confidence, and Fear kills the Dreams. No Success can define being's Character, and no Failure can define being's Life. Do not be, a Saturnine, or a Noob in this game and the Show of the Life. Do not get riled by the words and deeds of others. Jealousy kills the Peace, and Ego kills the Growth. Many a times, the Life seems to hit a brick wall; do not get flummoxed. Become a show-stopper. Life is a Question, and how we live it, is its Answer. Have no anathemas. Life is great teacher; if we do not learn a lesson first time, it repeats it second time. Externally, the Nature and the Surroundings, and internally, the True Self, act as the Oracle. 17 Seconds of pure thoughts (pure energy) and undivided attention to an intention are tentamount to 2000 action hours by the Nature and the Universe to fulfil any intention of a being. 34 Seconds of pure thoughts (pure energy) and undivided attention to an intention are tentamount to 20000 action hours by the Nature and the Universe to fulfil any intention of a being. 68 Seconds (the highest level of normal beings) of pure thoughts (pure energy) and undivided attention to an intention are tentamount to 2 Lakhs action hours by the Nature and the Universe to fulfil any intention of a being.

CHAPTER FIFTEEN

Bhagyank 5

Bhagyank 5 is the Number of Wisdom and Luck. Number 5 is ruled by the planet Mercury. Planet Mercury is the king of all planets. Planet Mercury eclipses other planets. Beings with Bhagyank 5 are very Lucky. Number 5 appears at the Centre position or the Middle of Number Sequence 1, 2, 3, 4, 5, 6, 7, 8 and 9.

Characteristics - Strengths and Weaknesses of Beings born with Bhagyank 5 are as follows:

Strengths:

Beings having Bhagyank 5 are Gentle, very Knowledgeable, Adventurous, Versatile, Adaptive, Sociable, Good Decision-makers, Problem-solvers, Independent, Resourceful, Agile, Physically Fit and Strong. They stay Calm & Positive. They are very Good Teachers. These beings gel well with the others, and can work quite efficiently as the team members.

Weaknesses:

Strengths of beings are also beings weaknesses. Beings having Bhagyank 5 are normally Flexible and Balanced, but at times, may become quite Stubborn. These beings are Restless, Impulsive, Indecisive and Inconsistent.

Friend-Number(s):

Beings having Bhagyank 5 are compatible and friendly with other beings having Bhagyank 1, 3, 4, 5, 6, 7, 8 and 9. Bhagyank 5 beings will always have good relationships with beings having Bhagyank 1, therefore they can marry each other, or become good friends or start and run a business in partnership. Bhagyank 5 beings inspire the beings having Bhagyank 1. Bhagyank 5 and 3 beings can marry each other and do some business in partnership. This combination is good and mutually beneficial. They help each other and enjoy company and good relationships. Bhagyank 5 and 4 beings can marry each other and do some business in partnership. This combination goes together and mutually works very well. They have very good understanding between themselves. Bhagyank 5 and 5 beings are very much compatible to one another. It is a very powerful combination. Bhagyank 5 and 5 beings can become very good friends or even marry each other, and / or do some business in partnership. These beings, if work together, touch greater heights, and the pinnacles of success. Bhagyank 5 beings will always have good and beneficial relationships with beings having Bhagyank 6. It is an ideal combination. Therefore they can marry each other as they are quite compatible. They can be very good friends. Also, they can do some business in partnership. Bhagyank 5 and 7 beings exude cordiality in their relationships and produce much positive results by being together. They give positive energy to each other. They have good relationships. They are very good friends. They can marry each other, and also, do some business in partnership. Bhagyank 5 and 8 beings attract each other and can create a very good relationship. Both have positive vibrations and energy, therefore can go for any kind of relationship. They have good bonding and understanding. They can marry each other, and go for business partnership. Bhagyank 5 and 9 beings have positive vibrations and share good energy. Both are good for one another. Bhagyank 5 and 9 beings can enter into any kind of sweet and eternal and mutually beneficial relationship, whether marriage, or business partnership, or friendship, anything else. They can build a good understanding and bonding.

Anti-Number(s) and Remedies:

Beings having Bhagyank 5 are non-compatible and unfriendly with other beings having Bhagyank 2. Bhagyank 5 beings will always have bad relationships with beings having Bhagyank 2, and can never become good friends. Therefore, any kind of relationship between the Beings having Bhagyank 5 and 2 should be avoided.

Akashic Records give Remedies to the Problems of Life, which are created on the account of bad Karma of present Life and the past lives. Simplest Remedy is Forgiveness for mistakes. Meditation reveals, the Secrets of the Life, and of the Universe. Manifestation is the best Remedy. Changing the Mindset and Lifestyle are also very good Remedies.

Remedy(s) is/are to be done, for the Anti-Number(s), by pleasing these Anti-Number(s) associated Planet(s), as mentioned in the Chapter 1, or by pleasing the gods associated with these Planets by regular prayers, chanting and worshipping, or regular offerings to these Planets or the gods, or doing the right rituals everyday or right day(s), in order to placate them (associated Planets, associated gods), and make them happy.

Remedies-Beings having Bhagyank 5 must align themselves with the Mercury (Buddh). These Beings should use the Colour Green, as much as possible, in their Life. As recommended by the Vaastu, these Beings must keep Green Plants in the North (N) Direction of their

Office/House/Home. These Beings must do Meditation and Journaling for Introspection. After a little bit of Introspection, one is easily able to get to the bottom of any situation. Beings having Bhagyank 5 should wear Labradorite Crystal. Labradorite Crystals are revered for their mystical properties of Self-discovery, Intuition, and Spirit awakening. These beings need to take good care of their Healths. These Beings should keep Silver in their House/Home. Also, it is recommended that the Beings having Bhagyank 5 should practice "Active Listening". Active Listening refers to giving full attention and understanding to what other is saying, and then, responding suitably.

Best Career/Profession:

For Beings having Bhagyank 5, best Career or Profession are Lawyer, Astrology, Business, Head of the Organisation, Tours & Travels, Creativity, Fine Arts, Writer, Storytelling, and Production House.

Our Thoughts are the Cherry on the Cake of our whole Personality; an Epitome, a Ramrod. Do not be Waxy. The greatest Revenge is the Success. Always wish others, Godspeed for their Life's Journey. Do not be afraid of being mealy-mouthed, yet mince your words, for the self and the others, for the self-good and the others good. Have a devil-may-care attitude towards the Life.

CHAPTER SIXTEEN

Bhagyank 6

Bhagyank 6 is the Number of Wit & Intelligence, the Creativity, and the Self-confidence. Number 6 is ruled by the Planet Shukra or the Venus. Venus represents Knowledge, Kindness, Selflessness and the Love.

Characteristics - Strengths and Weaknesses of Beings born with Bhagyank 6 are as follows:

Strengths:

Beings having Bhagyank 6 are very Friendly. They are always there for you. They are quite Independent. They are Good at Conversation and Judgements. They love Travelling and enjoy their Life to its full. They are Epicurean. Women having Bhagyank 6 are Beautiful, Charming and Attractive, and look very Graceful in their old age. Beings with Bhagyank 6 are very Social beings and good Storytellers. They become very popular in their Lifetime. Beings having Bhagyank 5 are fond of Designs and the Arts.

Weaknesses:

Strengths of beings are also beings weaknesses. Beings having Bhagyank 6 are Atheist. They are the Rebels and Law-breakers. They are fond of insurrection. Beings having Bhagyank 6 have to work quite hard throughout their Life. They have big hearts, but don't translate into the Kindness.

Beautiful things intrigue such Beings.

Friend-Number(s):

Beings having Bhagyank 6 are compatible and friendly with other beings having Bhagyank 3, 4, 5, 8 and 9. Bhagyank 6 beings will always have good relationships with beings having Bhagyank 3; therefore they can marry each other, or become good friends or start and run a business in partnership. Bhagyank 6 and 4 beings can marry each other and do some business in partnership. This combination is good and mutually beneficial. They help each other and enjoy company and good relationships. Bhagyank 6 and 5 beings can marry each other and do some business in partnership. This combination goes together and mutually works very well. They have very good understanding between themselves. They are very good friends. Bhagyank 6 and 8 beings are compatible to one another. Bhagyank 6 and 8 beings can become very good friends or even marry each other, and / or do some business in partnership. Bhagyank 6 beings will always have good and beneficial relationships with beings having Bhagyank 9. It is an ideal combination. Therefore they can marry each other as they are quite compatible. They can be very good friends. Also, they can do some business in partnership.

Anti-Number(s) and Remedies:

Beings having Bhagyank 6 are non-compatible and unfriendly with other beings having Bhagyank 1, 2, 6 and 7. Bhagyank 6 beings will always have bad relationships with beings having Bhagyank 1, and can never become good friends. Therefore, any kind of relationship between the Beings having Bhagyank 6 and 1 should be avoided. Bhagyank 6 beings will always have bad relationships with beings having Bhagyank 2, and can never become good friends. Bhagyank 6 beings will always have bad relationships with other beings having Bhagyank 6, and can never become good friends. Bhagyank 6 beings will always have bad relationships with beings having Bhagyank 7, and can never become good friends. Therefore, they should avoid one another.

Akashic Records give Remedies to the Problems of Life, which are created on the account of bad Karma of present Life and the past lives. Simplest Remedy is Forgiveness for mistakes. Meditation reveals, the Secrets of the Life, and of the Universe. Manifestation is the best Remedy. Changing the Mindset and Lifestyle are also very good Remedies.

Remedy(s) is/are to be done, for the Anti-Number(s), by pleasing these Anti-Number(s) associated Planet(s), as mentioned in the Chapter 1, or by pleasing the gods associated with these Planets by regular prayers, chanting and worshipping, or regular offerings to these Planets or the gods, or doing the right rituals everyday or right day(s), in order to placate them (associated Planets, associated gods), and make them happy.

Remedies-Beings having Bhagyank 6 must align themselves with the Venus (Shukra). These Beings should use/keep Diamond, Jade and a Silver Coin engraved with Number 33. They should regularly /donate Milk, Milk Products and Sweets on Fridays. These Beings should decorate their Office/House/Home with symmetrical decor arrangements. It shall balance the energies. They should keep flower plants in their Office/House/Home. Also, Beings having Bhagyank 6 should take good care of Self, and especially their Diet (Sugar, Vitamin E).

Best Career/Profession:

For Beings having Bhagyank 6, best Career or Profession are Business & Commerce, Politics, Law. Entertainment, and Hotel Industry.

Hard becomes easy with right thinking, planning and the actions. Have no truck with bad beings in the Life. Be sanguine about every things associated with the self, and with the Life. Life is frigging awesome.

CHAPTER SEVENTEEN

Bhagyank 7

Bhagyank 7 is the Number of Knowledge, Understanding, being Practical, Creating, Seeking, Curiosity, Friendship and Introspection. Number 7 is ruled by the Ketu.

Characteristics - Strengths and Weaknesses of Beings born with Bhagyank 7 are as follows:

Strengths:

Beings having Bhagyank 7 are Inspirational to others in terms of their Thoughts and Actions. They are quite good at Conversation. They are Seekers, Smart, Practical, Dedicated, Hardworking, Generrous, Helpful, Spiritual, Ambitious, Curious, Intuitive, Logical, Creative, Empathetic, Explorers, Mystic, Sensitive, Emotional and quite Intelligent. They have good intellectual and analytical strengths. Beings with Bhagyank 7 are Sentimental beings. Also, they are Social beings with very Good Oratory Skills. They love Travelling and Enjoy their Life to its full. They are Noble, Graceful and Epicurean. Beings having Bhagyank 7 value Autonomy.

Weaknesses:

Strengths of beings are also beings weaknesses. Beings having Bhagyank 7 remain worried about the future. They are nervous and anxious beings. Such beings are overly skeptical. They often become prey of over-criticism. They prefer to live in isolation. They may become escapist. Beings having Bhagyank 7 face emotional challenges in the Life. They are Daydreamers.

Friend-Number(s):

Beings having Bhagyank 7 are compatible and friendly with other beings having Bhagyank 1, 2, 4 and 5. Bhagyank 7 and Bhagyank 1 beings are an ideal match. Bhagyank 7 beings will always have good relationship with beings having Bhagyank 1; therefore they can marry each other, or become good friends or start and run a business in partnership. Bhagyank 7 beings and Bhagyank 2 beings are in harmony to one another. They are very good friends. They maintain very good relationship throughout their life. Bhagyank 7 and 4 beings can marry each other and do some business in partnership. They have strong bonding. This combination is good and mutually beneficial. They help each other and enjoy each other's company and have very good relationship. Bhagyank 7 and 5 beings can marry each other and do some business in partnership. This combination goes together and mutually works very well. They have very good understanding between themselves. They are very good friends. They attract one another. They help each other and enjoy each other's company and have very good relationship.

Anti-Number(s) and Remedies:

Beings having Bhagyank 7 are non-compatible and unfriendly with other beings having Bhagyank 3, 6, 7, 8 and 9. Bhagyank 7 beings will always have bad relationships with beings having Bhagyank 3, and can never become good friends. Therefore, any kind of relationship between the Beings having Bhagyank 7 and 3 should be avoided. Their thinking are quite different. Bhagyank 7 beings will always have bad relationships with beings having Bhagyank

6, and can never become good friends. They do not help each other. Therefore, they should avoid each other. Bhagyank 7 beings will always have bad relationship with other beings having Bhagyank 7, and can never become good friends and can have good relationship. This is an anti-numbers combination. Bhagyank 7 beings will always have bad relationships with beings having Bhagyank 8, and can never become good friends. Therefore, they should avoid one another. Bhagyank 7 beings will always have bad relationships with beings having Bhagyank 9, and can never become good friends. Therefore, they should avoid one another.

Akashic Records give Remedies to the Problems of Life, which are created on the account of bad Karma of present Life and the past lives. Simplest Remedy is Forgiveness for mistakes. Meditation reveals, the Secrets of the Life, and of the Universe. Manifestation is the best Remedy. Changing the Mindset and Lifestyle are also very good Remedies.

Remedy(s) is/are to be done, for the Anti-Number(s), by pleasing these Anti-Number(s) associated Planet(s), as mentioned in the Chapter 1, or by pleasing the gods associated with these Planets by regular prayers, chanting and worshipping, or regular offerings to these Planets or the gods, or doing the right rituals everyday or right day(s), in order to placate them (associated Planets, associated gods), and make them happy.

Remedies-Beings having Bhagyank 7 must align themselves with the Neptune (Ketu). These Beings should worship Lord Ganesha, and also, circumambulate and worship Fig Tree (Peepal Tree or Ficus Religiosa). They should wear Cat's Eye Crystal. Cat's Eye Crystal is a grounding stone, which provides strong protective energy to the being. Cat's Eye Crystal dispels negative energy from the aura of the being. Cat's Eye Crystal amplifies good luck and fortune of the being having Bhagyank 7. Chrysoberyl Cat's Eye Crystal transforms being's negative energy into the positive energy. Cat's Eye Crystal brings confidence, optimism, happiness, serenity and the generosity. These Beings must invest in Gold and Silver), and use Gold and Silver utensils at their Office/House/Home. Beings having Bhagyank 7 should start their day with positive affirmation and do deep breathing.

Best Career/Profession:

For the Beings having Bhagyank 7, best Career or Profession are Occult (Spirit Hunting, Numerology, Palmistry, Astrology, Tarot Card Reading etc.) & the Spirituality, Agriculture, Photography and Teaching.

For the outside growth, inside growth is necessary. Universe bows down, and also surrenders, before a still mind. Do not be a highbrow. Discourage broaching. "Cat got your tongue" formula fits quite well in many situations of the Life, on the day-to-day basis. Life has ebb and flow pattern. Be a vanguard. Develop the ability to turn the tide. True Friends and True Love come naturally in the Life, without any planning and action.

CHAPTER EIGHTEEN

Bhagyank 8

Bhagyank 8 is the Number of Ambition, Resilience and the Power. Number 8 is ruled by the Saturn or the Shani. Beings having Bhagyank 8 like to spend time alone.

Characteristics - Strengths and Weaknesses of Beings born with Bhagyank 8 are as follows:

Strengths:

Beings having Bhagyank 6 are resolute beings with strong Willpower, Patience, Tolerance and the Endurance. They have the ability to extricate themselves from difficult and unfavourable situations of the Life. These beings are very Hardworking and Ambitious. They can organise the things very well. They excel in their Life, achieve the set Goals, and reach the pinnacle of their Career, if they have chosen the Best Career or the Profession, as recommended. In the later part of their Life, these beings get Success and Recognition. They remain very busy. Interestingly, these beings do not get stressed. Also, these beings do feel Burnout. Burnout is a state of emotional, physical, and mental exhaustion, which is caused by excessive and prolonged stress. Beings having Bhagyank 8 are Philanthropists, Good Planners, Good Storytellers and Good Conversationalists.

Weaknesses:

Strengths of beings are also beings weaknesses. Beings having Bhagyank 8 witness Loss, Unreasonable Delays and Unfavouarble Events in their Life. They face lots of Hardships, Challenges and Obstacles in their Life. Beings with Bhagyank 8 complain of Loneliness. Their Love Life can be Bottom-low. They live with the Fear of Rejection and Separation. They should feel Secure. They should give Time to their Relationships.

Friend-Number(s):

Beings having Bhagyank 8 are compatible and friendly with other beings having Bhagyank 2, 3, 5 and 6. Bhagyank 8 and Bhagyank 2 beings attract each other. Bhagyank 8 beings will always have good relationship with beings having Bhagyank 2; therefore they can marry each other, or become good friends or start and run a business in partnership. Bhagyank 8 beings and Bhagyank 3 beings are in harmony to one another. They can marry each other. They are very good friends. They maintain very good relationship throughout their life. Bhagyank 8 and 5 beings are good friends, can marry each other and do some business in partnership. They have strong bonding. This combination is good and mutually beneficial. They help each other and enjoy each other's company and have very good relationship. Bhagyank 8 and 6 beings can marry each other and do some business in partnership. This combination goes together and mutually works very well. They have very good understanding between themselves. They are very good friends. They attract one another. They help each other and enjoy each other's company and have very good bonding and relationship.

Anti-Number(s) and Remedies:

Beings having Bhagyank 8 are non-compatible and unfriendly with other beings having Bhagyank 1, 4, 7, 8 and 9. Bhagyank 8 beings will always have bad bonding and the relationship with beings having Bhagyank 1, and can never become good friends. Therefore, any kind of relationship between the Beings having Bhagyank 8 and 1 should be avoided. Their thinking are quite different. Bhagyank 8 beings will always have bad relationships with beings having Bhagyank 4, and can never become good friends. They do not help each other. Therefore, they should avoid each other. 8 and 4 is a bad combination. Bhagyank 8 beings will always have bad relationship with other beings having Bhagyank 7, and can never become good friends and can have good relationship. This is an anti-numbers combination. These numbers are not in harmony with one another. Bhagyank 8 beings will always have bad relationships with beings having Bhagyank 8, and can never become good friends. Therefore, they should avoid one another. This is an anti-numbers combination. Bhagyank 8 beings will always have bad relationships with beings having Bhagyank 9, and can never become good friends. Therefore, they should avoid one another. This is an anti-numbers combination.

Akashic Records give Remedies to the Problems of Life, which are created on the account of bad Karma of present Life and the past lives. Simplest Remedy is Forgiveness for mistakes. Meditation reveals, the Secrets of the Life, and of the Universe. Manifestation is the best Remedy. Changing the Mindset and Lifestyle are also very good Remedies.

Remedy(s) is/are to be done, for the Anti-Number(s), by pleasing these Anti-Number(s) associated Planet(s), as mentioned in the Chapter 1, or by pleasing the gods associated with these Planets by regular prayers, chanting and worshipping, or regular offerings to these Planets or the gods, or doing the right rituals everyday or right day(s), in order to placate them (associated Planets, associated gods), and make them happy.

Remedies-Beings having Bhagyank 8 must align themselves with the Saturn (Shani). These Beings should wear an Ashtadhatu (अष्टधात्/आठ धातुएँ: सोना, चाँदी, सीसा, ताँबा, राँगा, जस्ता, लोहा, पारा) Bangle for enhanced energy flow. They should wear Good Watch. Beings having Bhagyank 8 must lie on Earth. Frequent Massage is good for beings having Bhagyank 8. Beings having Bhagyank 8 should donate food.

Best Career/Profession:

For Beings having Bhagyank 8, best Career or Profession are Corporate Jobs, Banking & Commerce, Armed Forces, Judiciary, Trust and Charitable Oragnisations.

Silence is the Strength. Always use the uncommon nous in the Life. Life is not evenly paced. Our Life is the outcome of our thoughts. We create our Future and our Life. Our Beliefs and our Judgements create our Life's Reality. One's preparations, i.e. meeting the opportunity(s) are his or her Luck. Happy beings take their Life day-by-day and do not complain, and are thankful to every little thing in the Life. Do not be iniquitous and imperious in Life. No one-upmanship in Life. One day, our trappings will be left here only. Always, be in your element. Rarely, there is a three-peat in the Life. Life's precarity does not allow anyone to roar up on the others. Many things in the Life prove to be just the chimera.

Bhagyank 9

Bhagyank 9 is the Number of Art and the Beauty. Number 9 is ruled by the Planet Mars. Beings having Bhagyank 9 are quite Strong-willed, very Courageous and Effective Leaders. However, they get provoked, and become angry very easily, and then, start protesting even at the trifles.

Characteristics - Strengths and Weaknesses of Beings born with Bhagyank 9 are as follows:

Strengths:

Beings having Bhagyank 9 are quite Busy beings. They are very Hard Working beings. As a result of their hard work, they get Love, Appreciation, Recognition, and Name & Fame in their Life. They are very Successful in the Fields of Arts & Beauty. Beings having Bhagyank 9 are Philanthropists, Good Planners, Good Storytellers, and Good Conversationalists.

Weaknesses:

Strengths of beings are also beings weaknesses. Beings having Bhagyank 9 face lots of Difficulties & Conflicts, and witness Loss, Unreasonable Delays and Unfavourable Events in their Life. They face lots of Hardships, Challenges & Obstacles in their Life. Beings having Bhagyank 9 are very Egotistical, quite Opinionated, and also, Aggressive, and these negative attributes casts these beings in an

Unfavourable Light. Beings having Bhagyank 9 find Flaws in the Others.

Friend-Number(s):

Beings having Bhagyank 9 are compatible and friendly with other beings having Bhagyank 1, 2, 3, 4, 5, 6 and 9. Bhagyank 9 and Bhagyank 1 beings attract each other and have good bonding. Bhagyank 9 beings will always have good relationship with beings having Bhagyank 1; therefore they can marry each other, or become good friends or start and run a business in partnership. Bhagyank 9 beings and Bhagyank 2 beings are in harmony to one another. They are mutually beneficial. They can marry each other. They are very good friends. They maintain very good relationship throughout their life. They can run a business in the partnership. Bhagyank 9 and 3 beings are an ideal match for one another. They can become very good friends. They can marry each other and do some business in partnership. They have strong bonding. This combination is good and mutually favourable and beneficial. They help each other and enjoy each other's company and have very good relationship. Bhagyank 9 and Bhagyank 4 beings attract each other. Bhagyank 9 and 4 beings can marry each other and do some business in partnership. This combination goes together and mutually works very well. They have very good understanding between themselves. They are very good friends. They help each other and enjoy each other's company and have very good bonding and relationship. Bhagyank 9 beings will always have good relationship with beings having Bhagyank 5; therefore they can marry each other, or become good friends or start and run a business in partnership. Bhagyank 9 beings will always have good relationship with beings having Bhagyank 6; therefore they can marry each other, or become good friends or start and run a business in partnership. They will always live in harmony, i.e. in the state of balance, peace, and the coherence. Bhagyank 9 beings and other Bhagyank 9 beings are in harmony to one another. They are good friends for a very long time. They are mutually beneficial. They can marry each other. They are very good friends. They maintain very good relationship throughout their life. They can run a business in the partnership.

Anti-Number(s) and Remedies:

Beings having Bhagyank 9 are non-compatible and unfriendly with other beings having Bhagyank 7 and 8. Bhagyank 9 beings will always have bad bonding and the relationship with beings having Bhagyank 7, and can never become good friends. Therefore, any kind of relationship between the Beings having Bhagyank 9 and 7 should be avoided. Their thinking is quite different. They act as the enemies of each other. Bhagyank 9 beings will always have bad relationships with beings having Bhagyank 8, and can never become good friends. They do not help each other. Therefore, they should avoid each other. 9 and 8 is a bad combination, i.e. the anti-numbers combination.

Akashic Records give Remedies to the Problems of Life, which are created on the account of bad Karma of present Life and the past lives. Simplest Remedy is Forgiveness for mistakes. Meditation reveals, the Secrets of the Life, and of the Universe. Manifestation is the best Remedy. Changing the Mindset and Lifestyle are also very good Remedies.

Remedy(s) is/are to be done, for the Anti-Number(s), by pleasing these Anti-Number(s) associated Planet(s), as mentioned in the Chapter 1, or by pleasing the gods associated with these Planets by regular prayers, chanting and worshipping, or regular offerings to these Planets or the gods, or doing the right rituals everyday or right day(s), in order to placate them (associated Planets, associated gods), and make them happy.

Remedies-Beings having Bhagyank 9 must align themselves with the Mars (Mangal). These Beings should chant Mars Mantras, and strengthen their Fire element. Beings having Bhagyank 9 should, practise Forgiveness, do Humanitarian Works, and embark on a journey. Also, these beings must make changes in their routine in order to maintain their health and keep the body, mind and soul in good condition.

Best Career/Profession:

For Beings having Bhagyank 8, best Career or Profession are Arts (Music, Sculpture, Painting, Literature, Architecture, Performing, Film etc.), Beauty (Salon, Cosmetology, Boutique, Designer, Decorator etc.), Event Oragniser, Electrician, Banking & Commerce, Business, Writer, Philosopher, Diplomat and Dentist.

In the iffy and jiffy Life, internalize values of honesty and perseverance, for the self-good. In this Universe, laws are quite stern, severe and grim, and non-discriminatory, and those, who do bad to others, always get their just deserts; Law of Karma. Nothing is higgledy-piggledy. Do not pass on de trop remarks. Get the moxie. Do not feel tramelled by anything. Life throws gazillion opportunities. Bang-on with the right actions of self and others. Make a Living, to make the Life, and not to, prevent the Life. Travel feeds the Soul. Life's journey is best measured in terms of its Experiences, rather than, in terms of its Time. Never Argue, but Chime in, and just Explain, why you are Right. Do not do rigmarole and anything in a slipshod manner. Do not elicit solipsism and lack of self-awareness. Do not make a complete shambles of your Life. In the Journey of Life, we are wayfarers. In the Life, if there are Choices, Choose the

Best, and if, there are No Choices, then Do the Best.

CHAPTER TWENTY

Angel Numbers

11, 77, 222, 333, 111, 444, 555, 666, 888, 1111, 1212, 1313, 1717, 2323, 2332, 3232, 4444, 7777 etc. or such number patterns (especially, the triplets and the quartets) are called the Angel Numbers. Angel Numbers affect the Life. At the time of seeing an Angel Number, the Angels enter into the being's aura, and push him or her, towards though(s) and actions (s). Angel Numbers suggest about giving respect to the energy. Angel Numbers are suggesting or guiding in their nature, as well as appreciative of currently ongoing actions. Seeing the Angel Numbers is not a mere coincidence, but a nature's perfect synchrony. Angels show the path(s) to be followed, and if one is already on the right path, seeing a right Angel Number, is its validation. Angels Numbers, if acted upon for their meaning and sense, suggestions and the guidance, blunt the edge of sword of bad Karma. Angel Numbers are a part of the Angel Therapy. Angel Therapy is a non-denominational Spiritual Healing Method. Angel Therapy is getting attuned to the Angel World, and involves working with the managers of the Angel World, i.e. the Guardian Angel(s) and the Archangel(s). The Day and the Time, when these number patterns are seen or shown to us by the Angels, give an Angel Message or the Warning, for that Day and the Time.

These number patterns are shown to us by the Angels. Angel Numbers give message about improving the feminine energy, i.e. giving respect to females in the family and the workplace. Right side of the body (future) is associated with the Masculine Energy and Left side of the body (past) is associated with the Feminine Energy. The vibrations felt, either at the Right side or the Left side, give a message to balance the associated energy. Energies should be balanced. Energies may have to be released or received. A number and its patterns, as seen over minimum 40 days, is one's Angel Number.

All numbers from 1 to 9 are positive numbers. Numbers have their energies. 1 is the number of the Sun, i.e. the self, self-respect, self-esteem, leadership, meaning Independence, Career. 2 is the number of the Moon, i.e. feminine energy (mother, sister, wife etc.), meaning Togetherness. 3 is the number of the Jupiter or Guru, i.e. seeking divine guidance, meaning making a Team. 4 is the number of the Uranus or Rahu, i.e. family, meaning Structure, Career. 5 is the number of the Mercury or Buddha, i.e. own-growth, meaning Change. 6 is the number of Venus or Shukra, meaning Harmony. 7 is the number of Neptune or Ketu, meaning Isolation, Career, and Change. 8 is the number of the Saturn or Shani, meaning Patience. And, 9 is the number of the Mars, meaning Completion.

Seeing the number 0 and its repeated patterns mean, be in the present; do deep breathing. 1111 gives a message about taking the charge of the day. 1212 is for the parents and the family, and gives a message about talking to the parents of the family once. 111 or 444 or 777 or 7777 give a message about job going good or presently good going career. Seeing 2 and its repeat patterns give a very clear message about improving the Feminine Energy (Feeling,

Emotions and Quality), i.e. giving more respect to the females in the family and the environment. On New Moon, receive the Feminine Energy, and on Full Moon, release the Feminine Energy, i.e. crying, talking etc.. Seeing 3 and its repeat patterns like 33 or 3333 give a very clear message about finding a Guru, i.e. an Ascended Master. Ascended Masters are high vibration, enlightened Beings of love and the light. An Ascended Master is a person, who has achieved enlightenment. The Ascended Master is no longer required to live on the Earth, like the normal beings. Seeing 44 or its repeated patterns like 444 or 4444 is very auspicious. 4 is the main Angel Number. 4 signifies the extreme level, whether good of bad. 4 means square, i.e. completeness. 4 main aspects of the Life are Health, Money, Relationships and the Personal Life. 5 is a balancing number, signifying the middle path (the right path), a point in-between the materialism and the spirituality. Number 5 comes in the centre of 1 to 9. In the Life, Middle Path means a state of equanimity, i.e. Buddha. Middle Path involves recognizing the impermanence and interconnectedness of all things in this existence. Middle Path means, liberating the self, from the grip of desires. Number 5 means embracing a life of mindfulness and moderation. Seeing repeated patterns of number 5, viz. numbers 555 or 5555 means communication, learning something new, travelling abroad, house change etc.. Seeing repeated patterns of number 6, viz. numbers 666 or 6666 means, not doing the excess and getting aware of (as 666 number also means the Devil), spending time on self, good health, enjoyment, quality time with family and friends, luxury, travelling abroad, shopping, fast growth etc., for next 6 days or 6 weeks or 6 months or 6 years. Seeing repeated patterns of number 7 (most spiritual number), viz. numbers 777 or

7777 means, slowing down and doing one thing at a time, impending major changes (materialism to spirituality) in next 7 days or 7 weeks or 7 months or 7 years, and thus, changing the whole track of the Life (thoughts and actions). Seeing repeated patterns of number 8, viz. numbers 888 or 8888 means balancing the karma, completion, introspection, planning and moving forward good luck, good money and good fortune. 888 is called Lion's Portal or Lion's Gate Portal. On the Date, "8-8-2024", 888 (2024 = 2+0+2+4 = 8), the Universe had opened the Lion's Gate Portal. Manifest with full faith and dedication, whatever you wish for, at 8: 00 AM and / or at 8:00 PM, for 8 days, and the Universe will give that thing. 888 denotes abundance and prosperity and the financial success. 888 Angel Number magnifies the potential for manifesting wealth and abundance by perfectly aligning with the Lion's Gate Portal energies for new beginnings and the positive changes. Seeing repeated patterns of number 9, viz. numbers 999 or 9999 means the last remaining portion, aggression, expression, conversations, completion, i.e. complete the things.

Number 1176 is a very powerful Switch Word. Switch Words determine and alter the being's energy from one dimension to the other dimension. Switch Words have the ability to change, one's energies and the subconscious mind. Switch Words help in understanding, the energy and the personality. Switch Words, also help in locating the lost objects.

Green Colour is of Budha (बुध), i.e. planet Mercury. Green is the Colour of the Nature, i.e. Balance and the Changes to make. Colour Pink is related to the Heart, and Seeing or Wearing something. Keeping anything of Pink

Colour heralds a forthcoming good Change in Life.

Changing the Mindset and the Lifestyle are best Remedies in the Life. We ourselves, our Karma, Angels and the God, test us (the self) all the time. Difficulties are Life Lessons, and if these Lessons are being learnt properly, they take the beings towards a new and much better Life than before. Trust the Angels. There is always Victory of the Truth, i.e. Good over the Bad, in this Creation. Path of truthfulness is arduous, but the only path for the good present Life and good Afterlife. We all are the children of the God, and he will take care of us, however, we must make our best efforts always. Always have good Thoughts, and do good Actions. Believe in this Universe, and its Powers. God will Bless all of Us. Stay jocund. Do not get exposed to the gossip and contumely, only griff. Do not poke borax at anything. Duck out from such situations. Do not get sick, if beings dunk on you. Nature heralds the forthcoming changes. Heaven has a perfect plan for all of us. Live consciously and well-aware of every moment of this precious Life. Awareness brings Clarity of Thoughts and the Actions, and the purpose of Life is fulfilled. Mind is the Traffic of Thoughts, do the Mind Management with the help of Yoga and the Meditation, and Select your Route carefully. Sky is not the Limit, but Mind is the Limit.

Lo Shu Grid And The Numerology

The "Lo Shu Grid" or the "Lo Shu Square" is a historical Chinese Numerological Puzzle. It is a 3×3 Magic-Square. Lo Shu is a Legendary Turtle. Lo Shu grid is found on its Shell. Lo Shu Grid is the Horoscope (Kundali) of the Numerology.

Lo Shu Grid

4 : 9 : 2

3 : 5 : 7

8 : 1 : 6

Here, sum of each Row, each Column and each Diagonal is 15.

Here, 03 Horizontal Planes are

4-9-2: Mental Plane or Mind Plane,

3-5-7: Emotional Plane or Heart Plane or Soul Plane, and the

8-1-6: Practical Plane.

Here, 03 Vertical Planes are

4-3-8: Thought Plane or Vision Plane,

9-5-1: Will Plane, and the

2-7-6: Action Plane.

Here, 02 Diagonal Planes are

4-5-6: Golden Yog or Raj Yog (Name, Fame and Money; Super Success in Life) or the Success Plane-I, and the

2-5-8: Silver Yog or Rajat Yog or Property Yog (Name, Fame and Money along with Ups and Downs in the Life) or the Success Plane-II; it represents the Earth element

Constructing one's Lo Shu Grid, i.e. one's Birth Chart

Here is an example. Consider a Date of Birth 22/03/ 1997. Its Mulank is 4 (2+2 = 4), and the Bhagyank is 6 (2+2+0+3+1+9+9+7 = 33 = 3+3 = 6). Now, in the Lo Shu Grid, as shown above, fill, the Date of Birth, the Mulank and the Bhagyank. Lo Shu Grid in this case is as follows:

4 : 9, 9 : 2, 2

3 : -- : 7

-- : 1 : 6

In the above Lo Shu Grid, in this case, identify the missing number(s), and the completely missing plane(s). The Missing numbers are 5 and 8. There is no completely missing, Horizontal Plane, Vertical Plane and the Diagonal Plane. Due to the missing number(s), or the missing plane(s), the qualities of these numbers and planes will also remain missing from his or her Life and the Personality.

Missing Number(s), Missing Plane(s) and Remedy(s):

Remedy(s) is/are to be done, for the missing number(s) in the Lo Shu Grid, as their effects will also be missing in the present Life and the Personality. Remedy(s) is/are not to be done for the number(s), which is/are present in one's constructed Lo Shu Grid. Remedy(s) is/are to be done, by pleasing these missing number(s) associated Planet(s), as mentioned in the Chapter 1, or by pleasing the gods associated with these Planets by regular prayers and worshipping, or regular offerings to these Planets or the gods, or doing the right rituals everyday or right day(s), in order to placate them (associated Planets, associated gods), and make them happy.

Completely missing planes will have drastic negative effect(s) on the being's Life and the Personality.

Number 1 is the number of Sun (the King). Number 1 represents the Self-respect, Name, Fame, Career, Independence, Ambition, Determination, Planning, Self-reliance, Self-confidence and the Willpower. If Number 1 is missing, then its associated attributes, viz. Self-respect, Name, Fame, Independence, Ambition, Determination, Self-reliance, Self-confidence and the Willpower, will also be missing from his or her Life and the Personality. Such a being will be become Sycophant and People-pleaser. He or she will not get Recognition, Name & fame, and the Success of his or her efforts/works. Such a being, having number 1 as missing, will also have Poor Communication and the Bonding with the others. Also, he or she will be Non-assertive.

Remedy for missing Number 1 is keeping an Aquarium or a Fountain or anything with Water's dominance, in the North direction of the House/Home/Office, as the Number 1 represents the North direction and the Water element.

Number 2 is the number of the Moon (the Queen). Number 2 represents, Creativity, Imbalanced Emotions (either Over-emotional, or No emotions, i.e. completely Dispassionate), Sensitivity, Happiness, Togetherness, Beauty, Marriage, Adaptation, Initiation, Cooperation and the Diplomacy. If Number 2 is missing, then its associated attributes, viz. Creativity, Imbalanced Emotions, Sensitivity, Togetherness, Beauty, Adaptation, Initiation, Cooperation and the Diplomacy, will also be missing from one's Life and the Personality. Such a being will become Hardened and Callous.

Remedy for missing Number 2 is putting Sceneries of Mountains and Planes without any Waterbody, in the North direction of the House/Home/Office, as the Number 2 represents the South-West direction and the Earth element. Alternatively, to reduce the negative effects in the Life due to the missing Number 2, one can Donate White Clothes, or even White Colour Food items like Rice, Sugar etc..

Number 3 is the number of Jupiter, i.e. the Adviser. Jupiter calls for making the team(s). Number 3 represents, Wisdom (not Knowledge, but Street Smartness, i.e. knowing how to conduct in various situations), Education, Vision and Farsightedness and Decision-making, Creativity, Expressiveness, Growth, Health, Sociable, Storytelling and the Art. If Number 3 is missing, then its associated attributes, viz. Wisdom, Vision and Farsightedness and Decision-making, Creativity, Expressiveness, Growth, Sociable, Storytelling and Art, will also be missing from one's Life and the Personality. Such a being will have vacillating personality. He or She will also be a Goal-shifter, means changing the Rules or the Requirements of a Process or a Competition, while it's still in progress. He or She will not be able to make out, what to do. Such a being with Number 3 as missing will have Unstable Mind like a Markaṭa, i.e, a Monkey or an Ape, and will be not able to stick to one thing, in his or her Life. He or she will be a very poor Decision-maker.

Remedy for missing Number 3 is putting pictures of Woods, Forests, Plants etc., in the East direction of the House/Home/Office, as the Number 3 represents the East direction and the Wood element.

Number 4 is the number of Uranus or the Rahu. Uranus or Rahu represent Expansion and Structure. Number 4 represents Organisation, Planning, Vision, Hard Work, Discipline, Creativity, Practicality, Concentration, Persistence, Determination, Prosperity, Growth, Wealth, Independence and the Reliability. If Number 4 is missing, then Expansion and Organisation attributes will remain missing from the Life. Things move, but do not grow further, i.e. expand. Such a being with Number 4 as missing, is a Harum-scarum.

Remedy for missing Number 4 is using Wood based items like Pencil, Table and Chairs etc., Sports items like Cricket Bat, Wickets etc. as much as possible, and also, keeping the Wood items like Wood Rack in the East direction of the House/Home/Office, as the Number 4 represents the South-East direction and the Wood element.

Number 5 is the number of Mercury or Buddh, i.e. the Prince. Mercury is fastest moving planet. Buddh represents the Intellect, and the Change. Number 5 represents Freedom, Adaptation, Strength, Success, Flexibility, Communication, Balance & Stability, Focus & Determination, Motivation, Resilience, Curiosity and the Adventure. Other beings Like & Love such beings, having Number 5 in his or her Birth Chart. Beings having Number 5, are Business-minded, and also, Wealth-creators. Since, Number 5 is at the Centre of the Birth Chart, therefore, the Number 5 also denotes the Centre of the House or the Home. If Number 5 is missing, there will be Lack of Knowledge, and the Decision-making will be very poor. Life will be Unstable and Imbalanced.

Remedy for missing Number 5 is keeping Plants, Pictures of Stones, Rocks etc. without Water element, in the Centre of the House/Home/Office, or use the Quartz Crystal etc., as the Number 5 represents the Centre and the Earth element. Number 5 is connected to Green Colour.

Put and take care of Green Colour Plants at Office and Home. Use Green Colour in Outfits, Furnishings, Drapery, Food etc.. Make your Goals and do not be Indolent. Keep the Centre of the House tidy. Worship Lord Ganesha, who represents, Intelligence, Intellect and the Wisdom.

Number 6 is the number of Venus or Shukra, i.e. the Adviser. Venus represents Harmony, Love, Marriage, Wealth and the Luxury. Number 6 represents Peace, Help and Friendship, Compassion, Responsibility, Nurturing, Opportunity, Comfort, Luxury and Pleasure. Beings having Number 6 are Family-oriented beings. If Number 6 is missing, in one's personal Life, there will be lack of Love, and also, lack of Comfort & Luxury, despite good Earning.

Remedy for missing Number 6 is hanging long Wind Chimes, or putting Metal Artefacts preferably of Golden Colour, in the North-West direction of the House/Home, as the Number 6 represents the North-West direction and the Metal element. Alternatively, to reduce the negative effects in the Life due to the missing Number 6, one can also wear a Watch with a Golden Chain.

Number 7 is the number of Neptune or Ketu. Ketu represents Isolation. Number 7 stands for the Male child. Number 7 represents Child, Studies, Analyses, Mental activities, Research, Creativity, Opportunities, Introspection, Truth-seeking and the Spirituality. If Number 7 is missing, in one's personal Life, there will be Dissatisfaction and Emptiness and Vacuum. A being with Number 7 as missing, is not able to enjoy his or her Possessions. Enjoyment in the present moment will be greatly missing, if the Number 7 is missing.

Remedy for missing Number 7 is hanging long Wind Chimes in the West direction of the House/Home, as the Number 7 represents the West direction and the Metal element. Alternatively, to reduce the negative effects in the Life due to the missing Number 7, one can wear a Watch with a Silver Chain, and / or feed the dogs.

Number 8 is the Number of Saturn or Shani. Shani represents Patience. Number 8 represents Fame, Ambition, Justice, Hard work, Knowledge, Practicality, Memory, Consistency, Prosperity, Confidence and the Skill. Beings having Number 8 are Business-minded. If Number 8 is missing, in one's personal Life, there will be Struggle, lack of Hard Work and Consistency, many Ups and Downs in the Life, and Unnecessary Delays in various Activities and their Results. A being with Number 8 as missing, is not able to get the due Result(s), in proportion to his or her Hard Work.

Remedy for missing Number 8 is keeping Crystal and Water in the North-East direction of the House/Home/Office, as the Number 8 represents the North-East direction and the Earth element. Alternatively, to reduce the negative effects in the Life due to the missing Number 8, keep Fast on Saturday, and / or donate Salty Piquant Food Items.

Number 9 is the number of Mars, i.e. the Commander. Mars represents Completion. Number 9 represents Spunk (Courage and Determination), Valour, Energy, Empathy, Boldness, Motivation, Enthusiasm, Commitment, Recognition, Persistence, Uprightness, Exactitude, Name & Fame, Compassion and the Humanity, and Revenge also, very interestingly. Beings having Number 9 are ideal beings. If number 9 is missing, in one's personal Life, there will be lack of Enthusiasm. A being with Number 9 as missing will be Saturnine, i.e. always be demotivated, and also, feeling Lazy, most of the times; Spark will be missing from his or her Life.

Remedy for missing Number 9 is hang Pictures of Fire or glowing Bulb or similar looking things in the South direction of the House/Home/Office, as the Number 9 represents the South direction and the Fire element. Alternatively, to reduce the negative effects in the Life due to the missing Number 9, donate Red Lentils.

If the First Horizontal Plane, 4-9-2, i.e. the Mental Plane or the Mind Plane, is completely missing, then Memory of such a being will be poor. There will be Lack of Concentration, Understanding, and Retention of Things.

Remedy for the completely or partially missing First Horizontal Plane, 4-9-2, i.e. the Mental Plane or the Mind Plane, is same as the remedy for missing, all or few or one number(s), of this plane, which make(s) or complete(s) it.

If the Second Horizontal Plane, 3-5-7, i.e. the Emotional Plane or the Heart Plane or the Soul Plane is completely missing, then emotions will be missing, quite similar to the effects of missing Number 2. Such a being with Second Horizontal Plane, 3-5-7, i.e. the Emotional Plane or the Heart Plane or the Soul Plane completely missing, will be a dissatisfied being in his or her Life, and he or she will not be able to live in the present moment of the Life. Such a being with Second Horizontal Plane, 3-5-7, i.e. the Emotional Plane or the Heart Plane or the Soul Plane completely missing, will always feel thing(s) missing from his or her Life. Beings having this 3-5-7, i.e. the Emotional Plane or the Heart Plane or the Soul Plane are precisely Emotional Fools in the practical words, as these beings have hearts ruling over their heads, i.e. these beings think from their hearts and not from the brains, and are being befooled and ditched and duped again and again by bad beings for money or other helps.

Remedy for the completely or partially missing Second Horizontal Plane, 3-5-7, i.e. the Emotional Plane or the Heart Plane or the Soul Plane, is same as the remedy for missing, all or few or one number(s), of this plane, which make(s) or complete(s) it.

If the Third Horizontal Plane, 8-1-6, i.e. the Practical Plane, is completely missing, then there will be Struggles and Failures in the Life, things will get delayed, like, late results of actions, late success, and the element of luxury will remain missing from the Life. Such a being with Third Horizontal Plane, 8-1-6, i.e. the Practical Plane completely missing, will always look for the shortcuts in his or her Life, and then fails.

Remedy for the completely or partially missing Third Horizontal Plane, 8-1-6, i.e. the Practical Plane, is same as the remedy for missing, all or few or one number(s), of this plane, which make(s) or complete(s) it.

If the First Vertical Plane, 4-3-8, i.e. the Thought Plane or the Vision Plane, is completely missing, then one's, planning, organisational abilities and the decision making will be very poor, along with the lack of farsightedness and the vision. Such a being with First Vertical Plane, 4-3-8, i.e. the Thought Plane or the Vision Plane completely missing, will be a totally confused being, having no, goals and deadlines, for the things to be done. Such a being with First Vertical Plane, 4-3-8, i.e. the Thought Plane or the Vision Plane completely missing, is not taken seriously by the other beings.

Remedy for the completely or partially missing First Vertical Plane, 4-3-8, i.e. the Thought Plane or the Vision Plane is same as the remedy for missing, all or few or one number(s), of this plane, which make(s) or complete(s) it.

If the Second Vertical Plane, 9-5-1, i.e. the Will Plane, is completely missing, then one's, Self-respect, Courage & Valour, Resilience, Enthusiasm, Commitment and the Willpower will be either very poor or simply missing. Such a being with Second Vertical Plane, 9-5-1, i.e. the Will Plane, completely missing, will be an indolent being, having lack of motivation. Such a being with Second Vertical Plane, 9-5-1, i.e. the Will Plane, completely missing, is very easily susceptible to depression, due to repeated failures in his or her Life, and lack of willpower. Such a being with Second Vertical Plane, 9-5-1, i.e. the Will Plane, completely missing, becomes, sycophant and people-pleaser.

Remedy for the completely or partially missing Second Vertical Plane, 9-5-1, i.e. the Will Plane, is same as the remedy for missing, all or few or one number(s), of this plane, which make(s) or complete(s) it.

If the Third Vertical Plane, 2-7-6, i.e. the Action Plane, is completely missing, then execution and implementation of things is very poor. Such a being with Third Vertical Plane, 2-7-6, i.e. the Action Plane missing, is lazy being with poor health like weak digestion, and leaves the things midway, i.e. starts the things, but does not complete them.

Remedy for the completely or partially missing Third Vertical Plane, 2-7-6, i.e. the Action Plane, is same as the remedy for missing, all or few or one number(s), of this plane, which make(s) or complete(s) it.

If the First Diagonal Plane, 4-5-6, i.e. the Golden Yog or the Raj Yog or the Success Plane-I, is completely missing, then one's support system will be missing from his or her Life. Such a being, having this First Diagonal Plane, 4-5-6, i.e. the Golden Yog or Raj Yog or the Success Plane-I, in his or her Birth Chart, i.e. the Lo Shu Grid, is a Self-achiever, and he or she does not get support of others. A Self-achiever is always motivated enough to accomplish something important, and makes a difference in his or her and other beings lives. Self-achievers are known for their Ambitions and Orientation towards their Life's goal(s). Self-achievers are strategic communicators, and do not trust others, as many other beings had/have backstabbed them, in their Life. Self-achievers are known for the Excellence, very strong Leadership, intense drive, and very high Performance. Self-achievers cannot be befooled easily. Only 2-3% of beings are blessed with First Diagonal Plane, 4-5-6, i.e. the Golden Yog or Raj Yog or the Success Plane-I, being present in their Birth Chart or the Lo Shu Grid.

Remedy for the completely or partially missing First Diagonal Plane, 4-5-6, i.e. the Golden Yog or the Raj Yog or the Success Plane-I, is same as the remedy for missing, all or few or one number(s), of this plane, which make(s) or complete(s) it.

If the Second Diagonal Plane, 2-5-8, i.e. the Silver Yog or the Rajat Yog or the Property Yog or the Success Plane-II, is completely missing, then frustration will engulf the being, he or she will face many problems in the construction of their House/Home/Office.

Remedy for the completely or partially missing Second Diagonal Plane, 2-5-8, i.e. the Silver Yog or the Rajat Yog or the Property Yog or the Success Plane-II, is same as the remedy for missing, all or few or one number(s), of this plane, which make(s) or complete(s) it.

There are 03 Categories of Numbers in the Numerology, viz. Virtuous (सात्विकि), Majestic (राजसकि or रजोगुणी), and the Vengeful (तामसकि or तमोगुणी). Virtuous Numbers are 1, 3, 5 and 7. Majestic Numbers are 2 and 6. And, the Vengeful Numbers are 4, 8 and 9. If there are more Virtuous

Numbers in the Birth Chart, being is a much Better Soul, Lucky being and a Giver by Nature. If there are more Majestic Numbers in the Birth Chart, being are very practical in their approaches for everything in the Life. And, if there are more Vengeful Numbers in the Birth Chart, being will be full of Aggression, Anger and Ego, and such a being will remain occupied by negativity all the time. Thus, it is very important to balance the Birth Chart by remedies for the missing numbers and the planes in it.

Activate 1-5-9 for huge Success. Beings having these Numbers are Self-made and become King in their domains.

Vriddhi Rajyog beings, having Numbers 1, 5, 8 and 9 in their Birth Charts, are Big-hearted and Givers. The beings having Vriddhy Rajyog keep progressing, all throughout their Life, and write a Rags-to-Riches Story, i.e. from Zero to Hero, despite remaining surrounded by other jealous and envious beings. Such beings having Vriddhi Rajyog change the generations.

7th House of the Horoscope is of Marriage.

We all are Spiritual beings, getting human experiences. At the Physical Level, Life is "curate's egg". Our Life is the Product of our Decisions, and not the Circumstances. Present becomes the Future. Unrepeated unlearnt mistake is the only mistake; otherwise it is learning for the Life. Do not back-burner good actions. Good Karma is the golden goose. Life is a continuum, a ratiocination, and not a one-and-done process. Good Karma has the ability to turn the tide of misfortunes of Life. Good thoughts beef up the Quality of Life, and make the peace and the happiness arrive in the Life with the preternatural speed. Be active; do not put yourself in hypogeum. We all are God-Self dyad; the puissant beings. Tychism is operative in the cosmos. Do not get involved in casuistry and sophism. Nature is the greatest Artist, and creates all special effects in the Life, by juxtaposing light and dark sides of the Life. Do not talk about the bad past, as it is all the water under the bridge, now. We all are the habitué of this planet Earth. In the visuals of the Life, foreground and background bokeh both, are equally important. Good behaviour is a sure-fire way of earning good Karma. Tap into the rich store of the Universe. What looks simple and easy, is a bittersweet. What is Physical, is Chimera. The time, when one enters into the Spirituality, is the high point of his or her Life.

CHAPTER TWENTY-TWO

Name Number Numerology

Name should be compatible with the Date of Birth, i.e. with its Mulank and Bhagyank. Name has Power. Date of Birth is chosen by the God. Name should be in sync with the Date of Birth. Name and Date of Birth both, create vibrations. There are Vedic Numerology and Chaldean Numerology. Chaldean Numerology originated from Chaldean people of the ancient Babylonia. In the Chaldean Numerology, each letter is connected to a number, which holds a specific vibration, and is linked to an Astrological Planet. Calculating Chaldean Numerology using the Name, helps in understanding Life's, Goals, Personality, and the Purpose.

In the Chaldean Numerology, if the Total Sum of the Name equals a Master Number, that means, number is associated with, either struggle or success & achievements.

The numerical values, as recommended in the Vedic Numerology, are as follows:

A, I, J, Q, Y = 1
B, C, K, R = 2
G, L, S = 3
D, M, T = 4
N, E = 5

U, V, W, X = 6

O, Z = 7

F, H, P = 8

Number 9 is a Divine Number, as any Number, added to the Number 9, results in itself, i.e. the same Number. There are 26 English alphabets, which when added, gives 2 + 6 = 8, matching / mapped with 8 numbers from 1 to 8, as mentioned above.

Number 8 is a rewarding Number for Metals and Leather. Number 8 makes a being to go from rags to riches. Number 8 is creates controversies and legal complications. Number 8 is of the Planet Saturn, and is quite slow but a big number. Jupiter and Saturn in their sizes are bigger than the Earth. Our reference is Earth, as we all are living on the Earth. Mercury and Venus are smaller in their sizes than the Earth; therefore, Mercury and Venus are the fast Planets as compared to the Earth.

Number 5 is the number of good partnership and good relationship.

Number 4 is the number of test and struggles in the Life. Interestingly Number 4 also, like Number 8, makes a being to go from rags to riches. Beings having Number 4 face problems of loan(s) and debt(s) in their Life.

Number 1 is the Leader Number. Such a being having the Name Number or the Mulank or the Bhagyank as 1, has full potential to become Leader, in his or her chosen field(s).

The numerical values, as recommended in the Chaldean Numerology, are as follows:

A, I, J, Q, Y = 1

B, K, R = 2

C, G, L, S = 3

D, M, T = 4

E, H, N, X = 5

U, V, W = 6

O, Z = 7

F, P = 8

Surname is never changed, only, first name and the middle name(if) are changed to become compatible with the Date of Birth.

Three groups of numbers are, Group of numbers 1, 2, 4 and 7, i.e. (1, 2, 4, 7), Group of numbers 3, 6 and 9, i.e. (3, 6, 9), and the Group of numbers 5 and 8, i.e. (5, 8). Group of Numbers is also called as the Family of Numbers.

Group, "(1, 2, 4, 7)" is of Sun, Moon, Uranus (Rahu) and Neptune (Ketu). This Group of Numbers has the powers of Business, Startup and Innovation. As compared with 2 and 4, 1 and 7 are stronger numbers and better numbers. Number 1 is strongest, as it is of the Sun. Number 1 brings huge Success. Number 1 relates to the Energy. Number 2 is related to the Mother and the Nutrition. Number 4 relates to Medical and the Medicine.

In the Group, "(3, 6, 9)", 3 and 6 are stronger numbers, and also, better numbers. Number 3 is of the Planet Jupiter, i.e. the biggest planet in its size, and the number 6 is of the Planet Venus, the faster planet. Number 3 relates to Money and the Banks.

In the Group, "(5, 8)", number 5 is stronger number, and also, better number. Number 5 is of the Planet Mercury, which is a fast planet. Number 5 relates to new businesses.

For the Name compatibility with the Date of Birth, beings having their Mulank or Bhagyank in the Group 1, 2, 4 and 7, should have their name total, matching with any number in the same Group 1, 2, 4 and 7. Similar, should also with other Number Groups, i.e. For Name compatibility with the Date of Birth, beings having their Mulank or

Bhagyank in the Group 3, 6 and 9, should have their name total, matching with any number in the same Group 3, 6 and 9, and the beings having their Mulank or Bhagyank in the Group 5 and 8, should have their name total, matching with any number in the same Group 5 and 8. Name Total means the Number obtained after summing all the alphabets of the Name, e.g. while using the Vedic Numerology, for the name Vinit Baba, the Name Total or the Sum Total is 5 (17+6 = 23 = 2+3 =5); Vinit (6+1+5+1+4 = 17) and Baba (2+1+2+1 = 6). Let the Date of Birth of Vinit Baba is 22 March, 1997, then its Mulank is 4 (2+2=4). 5 and 4 are not lying in the same Number Group, ergo; Name is non-compatible with the Mulank. Bhagyank of Vinit Baba is 3 (2+2+3+1+9+9+7 = 30 = 3+0 =3). 5 and 3 are not lying in the same Number Group, ergo; Name is non-compatible with the Bhagyank, also. Let us take another name, Vibhav Baba. Its sum total is 3 (6+1+2+8+1+6+2+1+2+1 = 30 = 3+0 = 3). Let the Date of Birth of Vibhav Baba is 01 July, 2002, then its Mulank is 1 (0+1=1). 3 and 1 are again not lying in the same Number Group, ergo; Name is non-compatible with the Mulank. Bhagyank of Vibhav Baba is 3 (1+7+2+0+0+2 = 12 = 1+2 = 3). 3 and 3 are coinciding, i.e. the same Number Group, thus, Name Vibhav Baba is compatible with the Bhagyank.

Name Correction or the Name Analyses in the Name Numerology, is all about finding the Group of Numbers, in which one is lying, and then creating their compatibility, if it is does not exist, by the process of first or middle name(s) spelling change, also called as the Alignment. Simplest way for Name Correction is to add the Alphabet(s), and bring the sum to the desired compatible number and the Group. Surname is never corrected in Name Number Numerology. Name Correction is done according to the Bhagyank, more preferred over Mulank, and also, the Zodiac Sign. Try making either one Number Group, or two Number Groups strong. It may not be possible to make all three Number Groups strong. Correct the Name spelling, and bring its sum total to 5. In the Numerology, numbers 5 and 7 have no enemies. Number 5 appears in the Centre of the Lo Shu Grid, and it is a Well-balanced Number, and this Number 5 gets and gives energy, to and fro, other remaining numbers.

Number 5 being in the Centre of the Lo Shu Grid is also called as the Brahmasthan. It is "the Best Number", among and over all other numbers.

Beings having Number 4 are the Kings in their initial Life, and then, in the later part of their Life, they have a severe prolonged downfall, and become paupers. Number 4 is of Rahu, and changes its form(s). Number 4 is good actor (i.e. form-changer). Number 8, like the number 4, is the number of struggles. Number 7 is of intuition. Therefore, beings having Number 7 are very good Advisers in all the domains. Number 9 is the number of a Warrior, i.e. beyond the body. In today's context, number 9, also refers to the Artificial Intelligence.

Full family's names calculations should also be done, for a happy family state, better relationships, and compatibility among the family members, and for their brighter fortunes. Any business name or the name of the Company for job purpose should either coincide with Mulank or with the Bhagyank, but more preferably with the Mulank. For Business, 3, 5, 6 and 8 are the Lucky Numbers.

Mulank has greater impact on the Life up to 35 years of the age. Bhagyank or the Destiny Number gets active after the age of 35 years. Bhagyank or the Destiny Number has a much greater impact after 35 years of the age in the Life journey. Name Number should be compatible with the Bhagyank. If the Name Number is compatible with the Mulank, it is OK, but more preferred with the Bhagyank. Compatibility means falling in the same Group of numbers, i.e. (1, 2, 4, 7), or (3, 6, 9), or (5, 8). Activate the Group(s), in which one has, his or her, Name Number, the Mulank, and the Bhagyank, falling into. Compatibility of Name Number with Mulank and/or Bhagyank brings the Success in the Life; let it be the Job, or the Business.

Name, if compatible with the Zodiac Sign, also brings huge Success, Name & Fame. It is called as "Astro-Numerology". Every Zodiac Sign is governed by a Planet. Astrology and Numerology are not different, but the very same. Name should have a compatibility with the ruling Planet. Combination of Moon and Venus (Shukra) attracts money in the Life.

Add EE, OO and AA (repeated alphabets) in the Name's spelling for Energy Alignment and Healing, for better Energy and the Journey of Life, towards the God's created destiny. Name is the Mantra directly affecting the Aura and the Vibrations, as it is being spoken time after time. Change the Name, in order to witness the changes happening in the Life, thereafter. Carefully monitor the response, due to change in the energy, due to the Name Correction. Name creates the Attitude and the Persona. Name Number should preferably be aligned with the Birth Number, Destiny Number and the Zodiac Sign.

Invest in the Stocks in the Stock Market, whose sum, and the release of stock Year's sum, are either same, or lie in the same Number Group, for large Returns/Profits. Product Type of Company should match the ruling Planet characteristics for larger Returns/Profits.

We all have premonition of what the future might bring. We all are slacklining between two points of the Birth and the Death. Notwithstanding the adversities of the Life, the Life demands, a right Thinking, a right Planning, and the timely Execution. Adversities are the Tests of the Life. When there is bright Sun, it is the right time to repair the Roof. Weak beings take Revenge. Strong beings Forgive. And, the Intelligent beings simply Ignore. Beings will badmouth you a lot. Let some of the things remain unrequited in the Life. Back-burner few decisions and the actions in the Life, for overall peace and happiness in the Life. Trying stay ice-cool. Live up to one's billing. Do not reminisce, as Past, Present and Future are a single point in time, and all three are happening now simultaneously, in the time. No arguments, based on the retrodiction. We all are minuscule, in fact nothing in this infinite existence and infinite expanse. We do not know what will happen, why it will happen and when it will happen. God, if willing, can even use comets or any celestial body to terraform this Earth. Have no plaints of any kind in the Life. Do not bloviate an issue, as it's easy to dismiss all the discourse, simply as the chatter. With no display of uppity, send such beings to Coventry, which misbehave with you. We all are sui generis.

Mobile Phone Number Numerology

Mobile Phone number must be compatible with the Date of Birth of being. Since, the Mobile Phone(s) is the constant companion in the current time or the age; therefore it should definitely match the being's Personality Number. Mobile Phone Number has a much greater impact on one's Health, Job, Promotion, Wealth, Family, and the Overall Happiness. Even, the Password of the Mobile Phone matters a lot, and also, affects the Life. Sum total of Mobile Phone Number and/or the Password, should be a Friend-Number, and not an Anti-Number. Anti-Number will create struggles in being's Life. On the contrary, a Friend-Number removes the struggles from the Life.

For Mulank 1 beings, sum total of their Mobile Phone Number and/or the Password should be 1, or 2, or 3, or 5, or 7, or 9. Mobile Phone Number 1 represents Authority, Aggression, Power and the Leadership. Number 1 means the Planet Sun, or the Surya.

For the Mulank 2 beings, sum total of their Mobile Phone Number and/or the Password should be 1, or 3, or 4, or 5, or 7, or 8, or 9. Numbers 1 and 2 are made for each other. Sum total of Mobile Phone Number and/or the Password as 5 and 7, are also good for beings having Mulank 2. Mobile Phone Number 2 represents Peace, Partnership, Courtship, Power and the Creativity. Number 2 means the Planet Moon, or the Chandrama.

For Mulank 3 beings, sum total of their Mobile Phone Number and/or Password as 1 and 5 are recommended over its other Friend-Numbers. 6 or 7 as sum total of Mobile Phone Number and/or Password are not good for beings having Mulank 3. Combination 36 is very bad (36 का आंकडा); i.e. Guru and Shukra. Mobile Phone Number 3 represents Enthusiasm, Ambition, Power and the Creativity. Number 3 means the Planet Jupiter, or the Guru.

For Mulank 4 beings, sum total of their Mobile Phone Number and/or Password as 7, or 1, or 5, or 6 are recommended, in the given order of preference, as above. 3 or 8 as sum total of Mobile Phone Number and/or Password are not good for beings having Mulank 4. Mobile Phone Number 4 represents Power, Hard Work, Reliability and the Stability. Number 4 means the Planet Uranus, or the Rahu.

For Mulank 5 beings, sum total of their Mobile Phone Number and/or Password as 1, or 3, or 4, or 5, or 6, or 7, or 8, or 9 are recommended. Number 2 as the sum total of Mobile Phone Number and/or Password are/is not good for beings having Mulank 5. Mobile Phone Number 5 represents Freedom, Adaptability, Adventure and the Power. Number 5 means the Planet Mercury, or the Buddh.

For Mulank 6 beings, sum total of their Mobile Phone Number and/or Password as 3, or 4, or 5, or 8, or 9 are recommended. Numbers 1, or 2, or 3, or 6, or 7 as sum total of Mobile Phone Number and/or Password are not good for beings having Mulank 6. Mobile Phone Number 6 represents Balance, Harmony, Compassion and the Power. Number 6 means the Planet Venus, or the Shukra.

For Mulank 7 beings, sum total of their Mobile Phone Number and/or Password as 1, or 2, or 4, or 5 are recommended. Numbers 3, or 6, or 7, or 8, or 9 as the sum total of Mobile Phone Number and/or Password are not good for beings having Mulank 7. Mobile Phone Number 7 represents Balance, Harmony, Compassion and the power. Mobile number 7 represents Wisdom, Inner Strength, Analytics and the Power. Number 7 means the Planet Neptune, or the Ketu.

For Mulank 8 beings, sum total of their Mobile Phone Number and/or Password as 5 is recommended. For Mulank 8 beings, sum total of Mobile Phone Number and/ or Password as 1 is not recommended. Numbers 8, or 4, or 9, in this order of preference, left to right, are also not recommended as the sum total of Mobile Phone Number and/or Password for the being having Mulank 8. Mobile Phone Number 8 represents Ambition, Success, Achievements and the Power. Number 8 means the Planet Saturn, or the Shani.

For Mulank 9 beings, sum total of their Mobile Phone Number and/or Password as 1, or 2, or 3, or 4, or 5, or 6, or 9 is recommended. For Mulank 9 beings, sum total of Mobile Phone Number and/or Password as 7 or 8 are not recommended. Mobile Phone Number 9 represents Spirituality, Compassion, Humanitarianism and the Power. Number 9 means the Planet Mars, or the Mangal.

Mobile Phone Password Patterns (Visual representations of Passwords) should be directing upwards as we move or traverse the finger to unlock the Phone, and never directing downwards or crisscrossing. Pattern Cross means struggle in the Life. If it is a number Password, then it should be in the increasing order of the number values. Do not keep 0 in the Password. Preferably, Password should end at 5 or 6.

Screen Wallpaper should be, either the image of the God or the Photos of Parents or the Family, i.e. any such thing, which is supportive, and also, very lucky. Never take Mobile Phone to the Washroom, as doing so, will make one's Planet Rahu weak, i.e. weakening the effects of the planet Uranus on his or her Life. Make Rahu strong for Name, Fame and Money. Keep Washroom doors always closed. What is not in normal vision is the Rahu, like the Internet, Ceiling of the Room, Nostrils, Fingernails and Toenails, Ear Holes, Doors from outside etc.. Keep the things neat and clean, and well-maintained. Follow these simple remedies in the Life, for a happy Life.

Have Mobile Phone Number ending with the Angel Number 555. Number 5 is the most balanced number among all other numbers in the Numerology. In the number sequence from 1 up to 9, Number 5 appears in the middle. Angel Numbers 111 and 666, are also good numbers. Mobile Phone Number ending with 1616 or 6161 or 1166 or 6611 or 1661 or 6116 are good numbers, as summing these numbers gives 5, which a very good number. Do not have 2 or 4 or 8, and their combinations, as the ending numbers the mobile phone, as these are not good.

Mobile Phone Password should be a combination of the numbers, in the increasing order, or the ascending order, e.g. 2456. If possible, do not keep the Number 0 in the Password. Numbers in the Password may repeat, but the ascending order must be maintained, e.g. 24556. If inevitable, give a single Number 0 in the Password. Password should end with Number 5, or the Number 6, for its good effects in the Life.

Keep Mobile Phone(s), neat and clean. There should be no cracks or dents on the Mobile Phone. Green Colour as the Mobile Phone Cover is generally good for all except those beings, in whose Date of Birth, Number 5 is appearing more than once, e.g. 25/05/1971.

There are beings, as thick as two short planks. They will pull out plank. Ignore. Forgive, and then forget. Demonstrate, the human traits, virtues and the values of the highest order, and touch the lives of others, through your conduct. Relationships never die a Natural Death; they die due to, Ego, Attitude and Ignorance. Charm attracts, but the Skill connects. Humility works better than the arrogance. Bearing Defeat, without losing Heart, is Courage. Do not display la-di-da manners. Look for Simian Line or the Palmar Crease in your palm; it is the Line, which gets formed, when Head Line and Heart Line join, evincing that there is no conflict between the heart and the mind, i.e. single-mindedness. God exists in all his Creations. Occasionally, exercise Catharsis. Spiritual growth means Epigenetics, and it should be in the Gene Expression. Become a Cutie pie, and not a Weirdo. It's a piebald Life. Our body is the microcosm of the existence, i.e. the macrocosm. We are the hobbits. Do meditation on a regular basis, in order to avoid the effects of Geopathic Stress in the Life. Grow mellower with every passing moment of the Journey of Life. In the Life, try having no truck with negative beings. Life is too prized. Our Beliefs become our Realties of the Life. For a stable Life, work on Health, Wealth, and the Happiness. Do not get pretty wound up before an act; as there is always a silver lining. Avoid giving a knee-jerk reaction. There should never be a reaction, but always a response. Always, flesh out your plans and actions.

One really has to have work cut out to finish bad Karma. Impacts of Karma on the Life cannot be gainsaid. Life is walking or treading a tightrope. Many times, in the Journey of Life, we are in a tight spot. Live up to your billing. Firm yourself up before responding, in order to avoid botching it up. Be a Centrist. Humility always works better than the arrogance. Using a Phylogeny, find your group of lineages forming a clade. Life is a potluck. Do not let the situations and the circumstances cast a pall over the present moments of the Journey of Life. Steal your deal with the Universe. Have a steely resolve. Leave the habit of picking the holes. We are the Nabobs. Life has a whodunit script. One gets one's just deserts.

Study self-Akashic Records, i.e. the personal Book of Life. Akashic Records or the Cosmic Library or the Spiritual Database contains the information, knowledge and the experiences of the past, present and the future of the soul in this universe. For Akashic Record access, the techniques are Visualisation, Lucid Dreaming, Astral Travelling, Meditation, Palm Leaf Reading etc.. While reading the Akashic Records, trust the intuition and then, answers to various asked questions are presented to us in the forms of words, symbols and/or the images.

Also, practise Quantum Healing for Overall Wellness in the Life.

House Number Numerology And Vehicle Registration Number Numerology

Sum total of House's number, i.e. the "House Number" must be compatible with the Date of Birth of the owner of the House. Check the House's House Number, with the Friend-Number(s) or the compatible number(s), and the Anti-Number(s) or the non-compatible number(s) or enemy number(s). Friend Numbers are good, and Anti-Numbers are bad. Even the date of possession of the house, or shifting to the house, should match one's Date of Birth. House, whose House Number, i.e. the sum total of House's number, is either Number 5 or Number 7, is a very good House. Number 5 and 7 have no enemies. Number 5 is still better over the number 7. Number 5 should be made strong. Number 5 relates to the Intellect, Intelligence and the Wisdom. Number 5 denotes Balance and Stability. While finding the sum total of the House's number, i.e. its House Number, do not consider the number of the Floor or of the Tower, only consider the number of the House, e.g. in an Apartment, a flat has its number as 216, i.e. 2nd tower, 1st floor, and 6th number of the House there, ergo, the House Number is 6. Common numbers are not counted for finding the sum total of House Number. In the case of independent houses, bungalows, mansion, detached villas, all the numbers need to be added in order to find the sum total of the House Number. Any common number, if appearing, has not to be counted for finding the sum total of House Number.

House, whose House Number, i.e. the sum total of House's number is Number 1, is a very good and lucky House. In this House, having the House Number 1, there will be frequent party(s), function(s) and the ceremony(s). Number 1 is the number of Sun (Surya). Numbers 1 and 8 are anti-numbers, ergo beings having their Date of Birth numbers as 8, 17 and 26 should not purchase or live in the House, having the House Number as 1. House, whose House Number is Number 1, is filled with the vibrations of the Sun.

Households of House, whose House Number is Number 2, are quite emotional beings. The families, living in such a House, having House Number 2, are very much attached to each other, and over-care for one another, and also, they have mood swings. Mood Swing is a sudden or intense change in a being's emotional state. In the Lunar Cycle, as the Purnima (पूर्णिमा) or the Full Moon is approached, mood becomes better. In the Lunar Cycle, on Amavasya (अमावस) or the New Moon, mood is worst. In the Lunar Cycle, from the state of the Full Moon to state of the New Moon, mood keeps becoming bad, as Moon becomes black gradually. House, having House Number 2, is filled with the vibrations of the Moon. Moon likes Water.

Households of House, whose House Number is Number 3 are quite disciplined, and do limited talks. House, whose House Number is Number 3, is filled with the vibrations of the Jupiter or the Guru. House, having House Number 3, is a very good house, however, as an exception, a being, whose Date of Birth Number(s) is/are Number 3, should not purchase or live in the House, having the House Number 3. However, for the teachers, the House, having its House Number 3, is very good, and also, lucky.

Households of House, whose House Number is Number 4, are quite logical, like the IT sector professionals. House, whose House Number is Number 4, is filled with the vibrations of the Uranus or the Rahu. Beings, whose Date of Birth number(s) is/are Number 4, should live in the Grey or White Colour house, having the House Number 4, having the direction South-West (SW), and the main gate or main door in the South or West directions, and there should be no waterlogging in the front of the House. Rahu does not like Water. Beings, who live in the House, having House Number 4, are not money spending. Number 4 is the Number of Brain (logic, reasoning etc.). Numbers 13 and 31 House Number houses usually do not exist. Numbers 13 and 31 both are Karmic Numbers. According to the Pythagorean Numerology, the Karmic Number (s) is/are the Alpha-Numeric Number(s), which is/are missing in the being's Name. Karmic Number (s) is/are the Lessons in the Life. Avoid Numbers 13 and 31 House Number houses. However, as an exception, if the Universe supports and permits, then the households of house with House Number 4, have phenomenal and exceptional growth.

Households of House Number 5, are kiddish or childish. House, whose House Number is Number 5, is filled with the vibrations of the Planet Mercury or the Buddh. Planet Buddh is a child planet. House Number 5, is a very good and very lucky house to live. House Number 5, is the house of, peace, good relationships, happiness, success, wealth and prosperity.

Households of House Number 6, keep their House very beautiful, and they get lots of name & fame, and money, while residing in this House. House, whose House Number is Number 6, is filled with the vibrations of the Planet Venus or the Shukra.

Households of House Number 7, are quite religious and also spiritual, and love touring and travelling. Households of House, whose House Number is Number 7, travel abroad. House, whose House Number is Number 7, is filled with the vibrations of the Planet Neptune or the Ketu. Number 7 beings have skin issues. Plaster of the House, having House Number 7 will keep getting peeled-off.

Households of House, whose House Number is Number 8, should worship Lord Hanuman. Chant Hanuman Chalisa. Lord Hanuman is also known as the Maruti, or the Bajrangabali, or the Anjaneya. Lord Hanuman is a deity in the Hinduism. Lord Hanuman is being revered as a divine Vanara (i.e. monkey). Lord Hanuman is a devoted companion of the deity Lord Rama. House, whose House Number is Number 8, is filled with the vibrations of the Planet Saturn, or the Shani. Usually, beings do not buy or occupy a House, whose House Number is 8. However, House Number 8 is fine for commercial purposes. Number 8 as the House Number is not recommended for living. Interestingly, House having the House Number 8, brings lots of money, but always worship the Lord Hanuman. Number 8 is the number of delay, but works will be surely done.

House with House Number 9, either will be a corner house or a house with lots of open spaces in its surroundings. The Number 9 comes at the last of the number series of the Numerology. House with House Number 9 is good for beings in the politics or in the administrative jobs. House Number 9 is filled with the vibrations of the Planet Mars or the Mangal.

Avoid House(s) having House Numbers as the Numbers 4 or 8. Vaastu of the house must be very good of overall well-being. Take a dog to the house, in order to check the Vaastu of that house, and if the dog is happy in that house, then Vaastu of the house is good; purchase or live in that house. Take toddler(s) to the house, in order to check the Vaastu of that house, and if toddler is happy, Vaastu of the house is good; purchase or live in that house. Balance the East, West, North and South directions for good Vaastu.

Sum total of Vehicle's Registration Number must also be compatible with the Date of Birth of the owner of the vehicle for a happy Life. Vehicle Registration Number, whose sum total of last 4 numbers is Number 1, will be driven more, and will never have natural accident. Number 1 is the number or Sun. Vehicle Registration Number, whose sum total of last 4 numbers is Number 2, will be driven more, without purpose. Number 2 is the number of the Moon. Vehicle Registration Number, whose sum total of last 4 numbers is Number 3, will be driven less, and always with purpose. Number 3 is the number of the Jupiter. Vehicle Registration Number, whose sum total of last 4 numbers is Number 4 should be driven for commercial purposes, and not for the home or the personal use. Such a vehicle, whose registration number's sum total of last 4 numbers is Number 4, will be used a lot, brings a lot of money, and has no natural accidents. It is good for trucks, lorries, cabs etc.. Number 4 is the number of the Uranus (Rahu). Vehicle Registration Number, whose sum total of last 4 numbers is Number 6 will be well-maintained by its owner or the user. Number 6 is the number of the Venus (Shukra). Vehicle Registration Number, whose sum total of last 4 numbers is Number 7, will be used for travel to the religious places, and in case, if it goes for the repair and maintenance, then it will remain in the Workshop or the Garage for a longer time, due to one reason or another, say non-availability of needed part(s). Number 7 is the number of Neptune (Ketu). Number 7 is a spiritual number. Vehicle Registration Number, whose sum total of last 4 numbers is Number 8 should be driven for commercial purposes, especially iron business, and not for the home. Such a vehicle, whose registration number's sum total of last 4 numbers is Number 8, will be used a lot, brings a lot of money, and has no natural accidents. It is good for trucks, lorries, cabs etc.. Number 8 is the number of the Saturn (Shani). Vehicle Registration Number, whose sum total of last 4 numbers is Number 9, will be / should be, of Red or Rust or Orange Colour, i.e. the Colour of Mars (the ruling planet of Number 9). Vehicle Registration Number, whose sum total of last 4 numbers is Number 9 is good for commercial purposes. Vehicle Registration Number, whose sum total of last 4 numbers is Number 9 will have frequent breakdowns, often due to the wiring issues/problems. Number 9 is the Number of Mars (Mangal).

Luck can never replace the Karma, i.e. the Work, the Hard Work. But, the Luck has an important role to play in almost everything in the Life. A mix of both, viz. the Luck and the Karma, definitely brings huge success. Look for the number written in the 9th house of the Horoscope. The 9th House of the Horoscope is connected with academic matters, law and courts, imaginative literature, and moral and ethical matters. The 9th House of the Horoscope represents the belief systems, the higher learning, the personal philosophy, exploration, and the intellect. Use remedies for this Number, if not compatible, written in the 9th house of the Horoscope, for activating the Luck in the Life, and becoming sanguine about the future Life.

One's future is the outcome of his or her today's decisions. Life is replete with godsends. Our diet in the Life is not only what we eat, but, what we see, what we listen, what we read, and with whom, we stay or live for the shorter or the longer periods of the Life. We should be physically, emotionally and spiritually mindful of the things, which we are putting or taking inside our bodies. Do not get led by the hubris. Develop the horse sense through spiritual practices. To live happy, attach yourself to the goals, and not to the things, or the beings. Zone yourself out from a situation or a place, where you are not feeling good, and thereafter, ensconce yourself in a much comfy environment of your choice. Refrain and restrain the self from ECG, i.e. Exaggeration, Complaint and Gossiping. Live to Give. Other beings will put you on the spot; avoid it, ignore it. Stating simply, "One Life is not enough".

Can Money buy the Happiness? Think...

CHAPTER TWENTY-FIVE

Books By Dr. Yaduvir Singh

This Book on the Numerology, containing the magical and the mysterious World of Numbers, is perfectly fitting in your hands; dang, not knowing it.

Other 14 best-sellers (Books) on Life Engineering (Spirituality) and Cartoon genres by Dr. Yaduvir Singh are "Cartoons 2021, 2022 & 2023", "Pyramid-Spiritual Journey Companion", "The Secret of Happiness", "Beyond the Blood", "Power of Positive Thinking", "Becoming Rich", "Power of Subconscious Mind", The Ghost", "2020 & 2021 The Cartoon Book", "Tere Bina-Without You", "Experiencing the God", "Himalaya-The Spiritual Abode", "Death-Demystified", and "Life-A Continuous Journey".

All these, 15 Books, are very easily accessible, and also, available on e-commerce platforms, Amazon, Flipkart, and others, and the Bookstores.